OTHER TITLES FROM BEACON & QUILL PUBLISHING

 Companion Guide for Parents & Mentors to The Ultimate Devotional for Teen Boys

 The Ultimate Devotional for Busy Men: Short Daily Readings about Men in the Bible to Help Focus Your Thoughts, Generate Reflection, and Allow the Holy Spirit to Work in You as You Enter the Busyness of Your Day

 Adulting Like a Boss: Life Skills for Tweens, Teens, and Young Adults (and Some Adults). Learn about Personal Finance, Time Management, Household Maintenance, and so Much More

To Be Released in 2025:

The Ultimate Devotional for Teen Girls

The Ultimate Devotional for Busy Women

A Fresh Look at Christian Doctrine

The God of the Old Testament

BEACON & QUILL
PUBLISHING LLC.

The Ultimate Devotional for Teen Boys

David Powell

BEACON & QUILL PUBLISHING LLC

CONTENTS

INTRODUCTION

As a father of three adult children — two daughters and a son — who all love and serve the Lord, I have seen firsthand the incredible journey of growing in faith. Watching my own children walk with Christ has been one of the greatest joys of my life. Over the years, God has given me the privilege of not only raising a family but also serving as a youth pastor. I've had the honor of leading mission trips to various countries and witnessing young people step out of their comfort zones to share God's love. These experiences have deeply inspired me to encourage more young people to grow in their relationship with God, and that inspiration is what led to the creation of this devotional.

This 52-week journey is designed specifically for teen boys, to help you deepen your relationship with God, grow in character, and develop practical faith that shapes how you live, serve, and relate to others. The devotional is structured in a way that allows you to explore different aspects of your faith and walk with God one week at a time, breaking the journey into daily moments of reflection and growth.

Each week is broken down into five days of devotionals. At the beginning of each week, you will find a practical challenge to focus on for the week to help you grow in a specific area. Each day features a passage of Scripture, accompanied by a short reflection to help you connect the truth of God's Word to your everyday life. After the reflection, you will find a journal prompt question to help get you thinking. These journaling questions are suggestions only — feel free to use all, some, or none of them as you see fit. However, I do encourage you to get yourself a journal and journal weekly about what God is teaching you and how you're growing in your faith. Writing down your thoughts can be a powerful way to track your spiritual journey and reflect on how far God has brought you.

In addition, each week features a real-life story or quote from Christian missionaries, athletes, artists, or leaders to show how faith can be lived out in all areas of life. These examples serve as inspiration and encouragement, a reminder that you are part of a larger story of believers who are seeking to live for God in every season and situation.

Every week also ends with a prayer to help you bring your reflections, challenges, and hopes to God. My hope is that this devotional helps you not just learn more about God, but truly walk with Him daily, grow closer to Him, and be transformed into who He created you to be.

The journey of growing in faith is not always easy, but it is deeply rewarding. Each week is an opportunity to know God better, to grow in character, and to learn how to live out your faith in practical, life-changing ways. My prayer for you is that you'll embrace this year-long journey with an open heart and a desire to seek God with all your heart, soul, and mind.

I pray that you look forward to the weeks ahead and that you will see God guide, encourage, and strengthen you as you dive into His Word and experience the joy of walking with Him.

In Christ,

David Powell

PS - If you haven't already, consider finding a mentor who can join you on this journey with the *Companion Guide for Parents and Mentors to The Ultimate Devotional for Teen Boys*. Every journey is better when shared with a companion.

Week i

Who is God?

Practical Challenge

Get to know God better this week by reflecting on His character. Each day, take 5 minutes to think about one aspect of God (Creator, Holy, Loving, Just, or Personal). Write down one way you see this attribute of God in your daily life or in the world around you. Pray and ask God to reveal more of Himself to you in each of these areas.

Day 1: God is Creator

Scripture: *Genesis 1:1* - "In the beginning God created the heavens and the earth." (NLT)

Reflection: God is the ultimate artist. All the things you see — the stars, mountains, animals, and even you — were made by Him. God's creation shows His power and creativity. Knowing that you are part of God's beautiful creation gives your life purpose and value. If God put so much thought into designing such an intricate universe, He has a plan for your life too.

Journal Question: When you think about God as the Creator of everything, how does that change the way you see yourself and the world around you?

Day 2: God is Holy

Scripture: *Isaiah 6:3* - "They were calling out to each other, 'Holy, holy, holy is the Lord of Heaven's Armies! The whole earth is filled with his glory!'" (NLT)

Reflection: Holy means set apart, pure and perfect. Sometimes, we may feel unworthy to approach God because of His holiness. However, His holiness is not meant to intimidate us or push us away. Rather, by reflecting on His holiness, we recognize our need for Him. God's holiness should inspire us to draw near to Him in worship and in reverence.

Journal Question: How do you respond to the idea of God being completely holy and pure? Does it inspire awe, fear, or something else?

Day 3: God is Loving

Scripture: *1 John 4:8* - "But anyone who does not love does not know God, for God is love." (NLT)

Reflection: God's love is not just something He shows, but *who He is.* His love is unconditional, sacrificial, and all-encompassing. He loves every part of you — even the parts you find difficult to love yourself. Nothing you can do will change God's love for you because it is not dependent on you; it is an unchanging piece of Himself. His love motivates us to love Him back and to love others as well.

Journal Question: How have you experienced God's love personally in your life? Is there anything in your life that would be different if you were able to truly embrace that God loves you unconditionally?

Day 4: God is Just

Scripture: *Psalm 89:14* - "Righteousness and justice are the foundation of your throne; love and faithfulness go before you." (NIV)

Reflection: God's justice is rooted in His perfect character. He is fair and does what is right. While His justice sometimes means punishment for wrongdoing, it also means that He defends the helpless and sets all things right in the end. Understanding God's justice helps us to see the way He balances love and righteousness.

Journal Question: How does knowing that God is just and fair comfort you or challenge you in difficult situations? Think about a situation in your life where you would like to pray for God's justice to be made evident. Now think about a situation in your life where you want to act differently than you have because you recognize that God will judge you justly.

Day 5: Knowing God Personally

Scripture: *Jeremiah 29:13* - "You will seek me and find me when you seek me with all your heart." (NIV)

Reflection: God isn't just a distant ruler or a powerful being — He is a personal God who wants to connect with you. A relationship with Him is not just about rules and rituals; it's about knowing Him, talking to Him, and growing in love for Him every day. When you truly seek God, He promises that you will find Him.

Journal Question: What steps can you take to seek a more personal relationship with God?

Weekly Summary

We explored who God is this week — Creator, Holy, Loving, Just, and Personal. These attributes paint a picture of a God who is powerful yet approachable, just yet merciful. Understanding these facets of God helps you to know Him better and experience His love and guidance more deeply.

Real-Life Story

Eric Liddell: The Runner Who Honored God Eric Liddell was a famous athlete who is known for his faith and love for God. He is often remembered for saying, "God made me fast. And when I run, I feel His pleasure."

In the 1924 Olympics, he refused to run in the race he had trained for because it took place on a Sunday, and he wanted to honor God by keeping that day for rest. Instead, he competed in a different race, which he wasn't expected to win — and won gold! Liddell later went on to become a missionary in

China, where he continued to live out his faith by serving others. Eric's life reminds us that knowing who God is and desiring to honor Him and trust Him can strengthen us to make bold decisions that demonstrate His power to the world around us (Lidell, 2001).

Prayer

"Dear God, thank You for revealing who You are to me. Help me to understand You as my Creator, Holy, Loving, Just, and Personal. I want to know You more deeply and live in a way that honors who You are. Open my heart to experience more of You each day. Amen."

GOD'S LOVE FOR YOU

Practical Challenge

Every day this week, write down one way you see God's love in your life. It could be through a person, a circumstance, or something simple like nature. At the end of the week, review the list and thank God for each of these displays of His love.

Day 1: God's Love is Unconditional

Scripture: *Romans 5:7-9* - "Now, most people would not be willing to die for an upright person, though someone might perhaps be willing to die for a person who is especially good. But God showed his great love for us by sending Christ to die for us while we were still sinners. And since we have been made right in God's sight by the blood of Christ, he will certainly save us from God's condemnation." (NLT)

Reflection: God's love doesn't depend on what you do or don't do. Nothing you face or struggle with can separate you from His love. He already chose to lavish His love on you before you had any idea who He was or what kind of a sacrifice He was making for you. He gave His love before you could even think of doing something to try and deserve it. His love is constant, never changing, and fully accepting. This unconditional love gives us freedom to approach Him just as we are, knowing that He will always love us deeply.

Journal Question: Is there something in your life that makes you feel unworthy of God's love? If so, ask God to show you specifically what is keeping you from feeling worthy of His love, the root of that feeling, and when it first started. Now surrender it to Him. If needed, repent and ask God for forgiveness or forgive someone else, depending on the circumstance of when you first started thinking you weren't worthy of His love. Lastly, replace that lie with the truth of His love.

Day 2: Examples of God's Love in the Bible

Scripture: *John 3:16* - "For this is how God loved the world: He gave his one and only Son, so that everyone who believes in him will not perish but have eternal life." (NLT)

Reflection: The greatest example of God's love is Jesus' sacrifice on the cross. Jesus willingly gave up His life to offer forgiveness and eternal life to everyone who chooses to receive it. This act of love shows how far God was willing to go to have a relationship with you. God's love is sacrificial, selfless, and transformative.

Journal Question: How does Jesus' sacrifice impact your understanding of God's love?

Day 3: Recognizing God's Love in Everyday Life

Scripture: *Psalm 136:1* - "Give thanks to the Lord, for he is good! His faithful love endures forever." (NLT)

Reflection: God's love is not only evident in the big moments but also in the small, everyday details. Whether it's the beauty of a sunrise, the encouragement from a friend, or the peace in your heart, God's love is woven into your life in countless ways. Take time to recognize and thank Him for these daily signs of His love.

Journal Question: Can you think of specific examples from your life where you've seen God's love for you in action? How about some examples from this week?

Day 4: Accepting and Embracing God's Love

Scripture: *Ephesians 3:17-19* - "Then Christ will make his home in your hearts as you trust in him. Your roots will grow down into God's love and keep you strong. And may you have the power to understand, as all God's people should, how wide, how long, how high, and how deep his love is. May you experience the love of Christ, though it is too great to understand fully. Then you will be made complete with all the fullness of life and power that comes from God." (NLT)

Reflection: Accepting God's love means understanding that you don't have to earn it. God doesn't delight in you because of anything you do, but because of who He is. Embracing God's love allows you to let go of shame, fear, and insecurity. Let His love fill your heart so that you can live confidently and joyfully in His embrace.

Journal Question: What holds you back from fully accepting and embracing God's love? How can you hand that barrier over to the Lord?

Day 5: Responding to God's Love Through Faith and Action

Scripture: *1 John 4:19* - "We love because he first loved us." (NIV)

Reflection: God's love for us calls for a response. When we truly understand His love, it compels us to love Him back and show love to others. This love isn't just a feeling but an action — choosing to forgive, serve, and live in a way that reflects His love.

Journal Question: How can you respond to God's love in your actions and relationships this week?

Weekly Summary

This week, we explored the vastness of God's love — unconditional, sacrificial, evident in everyday life, and available for us to embrace. Understanding and accepting God's love leads us to respond in faith and love for others. His love gives our lives meaning, purpose, and direction.

Real-Life Story

Katie Davis Majors: A Heart for Loving Like Jesus Katie Davis Majors, author of *Kisses from Katie*, was an ordinary teenager who followed an extraordinary calling from God. At 18 years old, she moved to Uganda and eventually adopted 13 young girls while starting a ministry to serve the people in her community. Katie's life is a powerful example of living out God's love, compassion, and grace in action. She says, "I have learned that I will not change the world, Jesus will do that. I can, however, change the world for one person. And if one person sees the love of Christ in me, it is worth every minute." Katie's story reminds us that God's love is transformational and that He can use our lives to make a difference in others' lives through simple acts of love and obedience (Davis, 2012).

Prayer

"Father, thank You for Your unconditional love. Help me to recognize Your love every day and embrace it fully. Teach me how to respond in faith and love to You and to others. Let Your love change my heart and guide my actions. Amen."

WEEK 3

GOD AS A FATHER

Practical Challenge

Talk to God daily as you would to a loving Father. Share your worries, joys, and dreams with Him. If you struggle to see God as your Father, ask Him to reveal Himself to you as a good Father this week. Remember that you are His beloved child. If your ideas of God as a Father are different than seeing him as a "Daddy" – for example, you can only picture Him in heaven, distant, instead of close and very present, or you only picture Him as stern and judgemental instead of loving – ask God to reveal to you any misconceptions you may have and even the source of those misconceptions and then ask Him to help you replace those ideas with His truth.

Day 1: What it Means for God to be Our Heavenly Father

Scripture: *1 John 3:1* - "See how very much our Father loves us, for he calls us his children, and that is what we are! But the people who belong to this world don't recognize that we are God's children because they don't know him." (NLT)

Reflection: God isn't just a distant deity; He is a loving Father who wants to have a close relationship with you. He sees you as His child, which means you are loved, accepted, and treasured. Just as a good earthly father cares for his children, God watches over you with affection and provides for your needs.

Journal Question: How does thinking of God as your Father change the way you view your relationship with Him? Does it change how you talk with Him or act toward Him?

Day 2: Comparing God's Perfect Fatherhood with Human Fathers

Scripture: *Psalm 68:5* - "Father to the fatherless, defender of widows— this is God, whose dwelling is holy." (NLT)

Reflection: No human father is perfect. Some of you may have great relationships with your dads, while others may have had really difficult experiences. But God's fatherhood is different than your earthly father's — it's perfect, compassionate, and never failing. If you struggle to understand God as a Father because of your own experiences, know that He is the ideal Father who will never let you down or leave you.

Journal Question: How does your experience with your earthly father shape your view of God as a Father? Are there any thoughts or feelings you need to bring to God for healing?

Day 3: Trusting God's Fatherly Guidance

Scripture: *Proverbs 3:5-6* - "Trust in the Lord with all your heart; do not depend on your own understanding. Seek his will in all you do, and he will show you which path to take." (NLT)

Reflection: A loving father gives good advice, and God is no different. But trusting His guidance isn't always easy. When life is confusing or things don't go as planned, remember that God sees the bigger picture. Trusting Him means surrendering your own desire for understanding and following where He leads, knowing that He has good plans for you.

Journal Question: In what areas of your life do you find it difficult to trust God's guidance? Why?

Day 4: His Fatherly Love, Protection, and Provision

Scripture: *Matthew 6:26* - "Look at the birds. They don't plant or harvest or store food in barns, for your heavenly Father feeds them. And aren't you far more valuable to him than they are?" (NLT)

Reflection: God provides for His creation — and that includes you. From your daily needs to your deepest longings, God is looking out for you. His love means He will guide, protect, and care for you in every season of life. If He takes careful care of birds and flowers, you can trust that He will surely take care of you.

Journal Question: In what ways have you experienced God's provision and protection in your life?

Day 5: Living as a Beloved Child of God

Scripture: *Romans 8:15* - "So you have not received a spirit that makes you fearful slaves. Instead, you received God's Spirit when he adopted you as his own children. Now we call him, 'Abba, Father.'" (NLT)

Reflection: Being a child of God means living in freedom, not fear. The word "Abba" is an intimate term for "Father," like saying "Dad." It shows the closeness of the relationship God desires with you. Let knowing that you are a beloved son of God change the way you see yourself — not as worthless or as an outsider, but as part of God's family with full access to His love, strength, and guidance.

Journal Question: What does it mean for you to live as a beloved child of God? How might this change your daily life?

Weekly Summary

This week focused on seeing God as a loving Father who provides, guides, and cares for His children. Understanding God as a perfect Father helps us trust Him more deeply. It helps us live in His love without fear as we recognize ourselves as valued members of His family. No matter what your earthly father is like, God's fatherhood is perfect, personal, and constant for you.

Real-Life Story

Bilquis Sheikh: "I Dared to Call Him Father" Bilquis Sheikh was a Pakistani Muslim who had a life-changing encounter with God. In her book *"I Dared to Call Him Father,"* she describes how she came to understand God as a personal and loving Father instead of a distant, angry deity. This realization transformed her life, giving her courage and peace to leave behind her old life and culture to follow Jesus, even at the risk of death in a country hostile to Christianity.

One of her most challenging times came when she started openly living out her Christian faith, which included attending church and speaking about her newfound beliefs. News of her conversion quickly spread, causing outrage among her family members and others in her community. She received threats from influential figures, warning her to renounce her faith or face severe consequences. Even her own family distanced themselves, fearing social disgrace and reprisals from the community.

Bilquis was told that her life could be in danger if she continued as a Christian. On one occasion, she heard rumors of a planned attack on her home. Despite the risk, she decided to stay, placing her trust in God's protection. That night, she prayed fervently, asking God for peace and strength. She experienced a deep sense of calm that replaced her fear, feeling God's presence with her. Remarkably, the potential attackers did not carry out their plans that night. Those who had planned to harm her later reported feeling an unexplainable reluctance to go through with their intentions, as if they were held back by something unseen. Bilquis attributed this change of heart to God's intervention, believing that He had shielded her from harm that night. Bilquis later shared that this experience reaffirmed her faith and deepened her reliance on God's provision and protection. Bilquis' story teaches us that seeing God as "Father" can change everything — bringing us into a close, life-giving relationship with God and empowering us to live boldly (Sheikh, 1978).

Prayer

"Heavenly Father, thank You for loving me as Your child. Help me to see You as my perfect Father and to trust in Your guidance, provision, and love.

Heal any hurt I may have from my earthly experiences and teach me to walk confidently as Your beloved child. Amen."

WEEK 4

THE IMPORTANCE OF PRAYER

Practical Challenge

Set aside a specific time each day to pray this week. Even if it's just 5 minutes, make it a priority. Find a quiet place, turn off distractions, and talk to God about your day, your worries, and what you're thankful for.

Day 1: Why Prayer is Essential in Building a Relationship with God

Scripture: *Revelation 3:20* - "'Look! I stand at the door and knock. If you hear my voice and open the door, I will come in, and we will share a meal together as friends.'" (NLT)

Reflection: Just like any friendship, communication is the key to growing closer. Prayer is simply talking to God, sharing your thoughts, fears, and hopes, and listening for His response. It's how we build a close, personal relationship with Him. Through prayer, we connect our hearts to His and align ourselves with His will. Through prayer, we learn what kind of things are on God's mind and what's on His heart.

Journal Question: How has prayer impacted your relationship with God? How do you want to see it impact your relationship with Him moving forward?

Day 2: The Power of Prayer to Change Our Hearts and Circumstances

Scripture: *James 5:16* - "Therefore confess your sins to each other and pray for each other so that you may be healed. The prayer of a righteous person is powerful and effective." (NIV)

Reflection: Prayer has the power to change situations — but it also changes us. When we pray, we invite God to work in our hearts, shaping us to be more like Him. Sometimes, God will change the circumstances, but other times, He uses prayer to change our perspective, giving us peace and strength.

Journal Question: Have you experienced a situation where prayer changed either the circumstance or your perspective? What happened?

Day 3: Jesus' Example of a Prayerful Life

Scripture: *Luke 6:12* - "One day soon afterward Jesus went up on a mountain to pray, and he prayed to God all night." (NLT)

Reflection: Jesus often took time away from crowds and distractions to pray. He made spending time with His Father a priority, even when life was busy. In this Scripture He prays the entire night before choosing His disciples. His example shows us that no matter how hectic life gets, prayer is essential to our spiritual health and growth. If Jesus needed to pray, so do we.

Journal Question: What are some practical ways you can follow Jesus' example of making prayer a priority? Is there any important decision in your life that might require an extended time in prayer?

Day 4: How Prayer Strengthens Our Trust in God

Scripture: *Psalm 55:22* - "Cast your cares on the Lord and he will sustain you; he will never let the righteous be shaken." (NIV)

Reflection: Prayer is a way to give our worries and fears to God. When we pray and see God's faithfulness in response, our trust in Him grows. In prayer, we are reminded that we don't have to carry our burdens alone — we can give them to God, trusting that He will sustain and guide us.

Journal Question: What do you find most difficult about praying consistently? How can you give that barrier to the Lord?

Day 5: Making Prayer a Daily Habit

Scripture: *1 Thessalonians 5:17* - "pray without ceasing," (NKJV)

Reflection: Making prayer a daily habit doesn't mean praying all day, but staying connected with God throughout your day. Find small moments to talk to God — while you're getting ready in the morning, walking to school, or before you go to bed. Building a habit of prayer keeps you in constant connection with your Heavenly Father and helps you be more aware of His presence in your daily life.

Journal Question: What steps can you take to make prayer a more regular part of your day?

Weekly Summary

This week, we learned about the power and importance of prayer in building our relationship with God. Prayer changes our circumstances, changes our hearts, and helps us grow closer to God. It strengthens our trust in Him and connects us to His guidance and peace. Cultivating a daily habit of prayer keeps us anchored in His presence.

Real-Life Story

George Müller: A Life of Prayer George Müller was a Christian evangelist known for his dedication to prayer and trust in God. He took care of thousands of orphans in 19th-century England without ever asking for donations — he simply prayed for God to provide. And God always answered in amazing ways, often at the last moment! One famous story of God's miraculous provision in George Müller's life happened one morning when the orphanage had run out of food entirely. Müller gathered the children and staff together in the dining hall, and they prayed, thanking God for the food they were about to receive—even though there was none.

As they finished the prayer, there was a knock at the door. When Müller opened it, the local baker stood there, explaining that he had felt God leading him to bake extra bread for the orphanage in the early hours of the morning. He had brought plenty to feed everyone. Just as the bread was being handed out, there was another knock at the door. This time, it was the milkman. His cart had broken down right outside the orphanage, and he explained that the milk would spoil by the time he could get the cart fixed. So, he offered all the milk to the orphans for free. In that single morning, the orphans received both bread and milk—enough to satisfy everyone. This moment is one of the many times George Müller recorded instances of God's timely provision, made possible through prayer and faith. Müller's life is a powerful example of how prayer can change not only personal circumstances but also impact the lives of countless others (Müller, 1984).

Prayer

"Lord, thank You for the gift of prayer. Help me to make it a priority and to connect with You daily. Teach me to trust You more through prayer and to see Your hand at work in my life. Help me to follow Jesus' example and seek You in all things. Amen."

WEEK 5

HOW TO PRAY

Practical Challenge

Continue with the challenge from last week, but this week choose one time each day to spend 5-10 minutes in prayer using the ACTS model. Write down any thoughts or things you feel God speaking to you, and be sure to take a few moments in each prayer to listen for His voice.

Day 1: Understanding the Basics of Prayer (ACTS: Adoration, Confession, Thanksgiving, Supplication)

Scripture: *Matthew 6:9-13* - "Pray like this: Our Father in heaven, may your name be kept holy. May your Kingdom come soon. May your will be done on earth, as it is in heaven. Give us today the food we need, and forgive us our sins, as we have forgiven those who sin against us. And don't let us yield to temptation, but rescue us from the evil one." (NLT)

Reflection: Jesus gave His disciples an example of how to pray, often known as the Lord's Prayer. One model for prayer that you can use, which is based off of Jesus' example, is the ACTS model: **Adoration** (praising God), **Confession** (admitting our sins), **Thanksgiving** (thanking God), and **Supplication** (asking for our needs and the needs of others). This balanced approach helps us to connect with God in a meaningful way.

Journal Question: Which parts of the ACTS model for prayer have you already regularly been incorporating in your prayer life? Which aspects are newer to you? Are any of these aspects of prayer uncomfortable to you? Why do you think that is?

Day 2: Being Honest and Open with God in Prayer

Scripture: *Psalm 62:8* - "Trust in him at all times, you people; pour out your hearts to him, for God is our refuge." (NIV)

Reflection: God desires honesty in our prayers. You don't have to use fancy words or hide your true feelings. He wants you to pour out your heart, whether you're happy, sad, confused, or angry. Being real with God draws you closer to Him and allows Him to work in your life in a personal and powerful way.

Journal Question: What holds you back from being honest and open with God in prayer?

Day 3: Praying for Others — Intercessory Prayer

Scripture: *1 Timothy 2:1* - "I urge you, first of all, to pray for all people. Ask God to help them; intercede on their behalf, and give thanks for them." (NLT)

Reflection: Intercessory prayer is praying on behalf of others. When you lift up your friends, family, and even those you don't know, you partner with God to bring about His will in their lives. It shows love and care for those around you, and it gives you the opportunity to be a part of what God is doing in the world around you. Who can you pray for today?

Journal Question: Who are some people you can start praying for regularly?

Day 4: Listening for God's Response

Scripture: *John 10:27* - "My sheep listen to my voice; I know them, and they follow me." (NLT)

Reflection: Prayer isn't just talking to God — it's also listening. God wants to speak to you, whether through His Word, a still, small voice in your heart, or circumstances around you. Taking time to be quiet and listen is an important part of prayer. Ask God to help you recognize His voice today.

Journal Question: When you pray, do you find it easy or difficult to listen for God's response? Why? What could you do to make it easier for yourself to be quiet and listen as part of your prayer life?

Day 5: Finding Time for Prayer Amidst a Busy Life

Scripture: *Psalm 5:3* - "Listen to my voice in the morning, Lord. Each morning I bring my requests to you and wait expectantly." (NLT)

Reflection: Life can be busy, and finding time to pray may feel difficult. But setting aside intentional time, like in the morning before your day begins, can be powerful. Even a few minutes of quiet prayer can set the tone for your day and keep your heart aligned with God. Start small and let your prayer life grow.

Journal Question: What changes can you make to prioritize prayer in your daily routine?

Weekly Summary

This week, we learned practical ways to pray — using the ACTS model, being honest with God, praying for others, listening for His response, and finding time for prayer in our busy lives. Prayer isn't about perfection or special words but about connecting your heart to God's and growing in relationship with Him.

Real-Life Story

Brother Lawrence: Practicing the Presence of God Brother Lawrence, a monk in the 1600s, discovered the beauty of connecting with God through prayer in everyday life. In the monastic tradition he was a part of, there were designated times throughout the day where everyone in the monastery stopped what they were doing and went to the sanctuary to pray. However, Brother Lawrence found that he had his most profound encounters and conversations with the Lord when he began to develop the habit of "practicing the presence of God" throughout his day. He learned to pray all throughout his day, whether washing dishes or doing daily chores, and found that God would answer him and meet with him in all of those moments, not just in the sanctuary. His life is a reminder that prayer doesn't have to be limited to specific times but can be a continuous conversation with God, inviting Him into every part of our lives (Lawrence, 1982).

Prayer

"Lord, teach me to pray in a way that honors You and helps me grow closer to You. Help me to be honest in my prayers, to pray for others, and to make time for You in my daily life. Teach me how to listen to the things You want to say to me during my prayers. Let my prayers be a true reflection of my heart for You. Amen."

LISTENING TO GOD

Practical Challenge

Spend time in quiet prayer each day, asking God to speak to you and help you recognize His voice. Then, find one passage of Scripture to read and reflect on how God is speaking to you through it. Write down what you sense God saying and how you can apply it to your life.

Day 1: God Speaks Through His Word, the Bible

Scripture: *2 Timothy 3:16* - "All Scripture is inspired by God and is useful to teach us what is true and to make us realize what is wrong in our lives. It corrects us when we are wrong and teaches us to do what is right." (NLT)

Reflection: The Bible is God's main way of speaking to us. Every word is inspired by Him and is meant to guide, encourage, and teach us. When we read the Bible, we open our hearts to hear God's voice and learn His truth. Spending time in Scripture daily is crucial to hearing from God.

Journal Question: Has there been a time where something in the Bible stood out to you and felt like it was written just for the situation you were in at the moment?

Day 2: Recognizing God's Voice in Prayer

Scripture: *Romans 10:17* - "So then faith *comes* by hearing, and hearing by the word of God." (NKJV)

Reflection: Prayer is a conversation with God. When you pray, God wants to answer and speak to you. But recognizing His voice takes practice and patience. He often speaks to our hearts with peace, guidance, and impressions that line up with His Word. Keep your heart open and expect to hear from Him. Ask Him to teach you how to recognize His voice better.

Journal Question: When you pray, how do you recognize when God is speaking back to you? Have you ever had a time where you knew without a doubt that God was speaking to you? What happened?

Day 3: How God Uses People and Circumstances to Guide Us

Scripture: *Proverbs 11:14* - "Where *there is* no counsel, the people fall; But in the multitude of counselors *there is* safety." (NKJV)

Reflection: God often speaks through others — parents, mentors, pastors, or friends who know Him. He can also guide us through our circumstances, using life's events to teach and direct us. Pay attention to how God might be using the people and situations around you to point you toward His path.

Journal Question: Think of a time when God used a person or circumstance to guide you. What happened?

Day 4: The Role of the Holy Spirit in Helping Us Understand God's Will

Scripture: *John 16:13* - "But when he, the Spirit of truth, comes, he will guide you into all the truth. He will not speak on his own; he will speak only what he hears, and he will tell you what is yet to come." (NIV)

Reflection: The Holy Spirit, God's presence within believers, helps us understand God's will and guides us into all truth. When you have a relationship with Jesus, the Holy Spirit works in your heart to reveal God's desires, comfort you, and give you wisdom for life's decisions. Invite the Holy Spirit to lead you as you seek God's direction.

Journal Question: How has the Holy Spirit helped you make decisions or given you peace in difficult times? If you're not sure that you have seen the Holy Spirit work in your life in that way, ask God to make you more aware of His Holy Spirit helping you and guiding you.

Day 5: Being Open and Responsive to God's Direction

Scripture: *James 1:22* - "But don't just listen to God's word. You must do what it says. Otherwise, you are only fooling yourselves." (NLT)

Reflection: It's not enough to just hear God's voice — we must also respond and obey. Being open to God's direction means saying "yes" to whatever He asks, even when it's challenging. When you listen and obey and get to see God come through in ways you never could have expected, you grow in faith and align yourself with God's purpose for your life.

Journal Question: Are there any areas in your life where you know God is speaking, but you've been hesitant to obey? Why?

Weekly Summary

This week, we focused on listening to God through His Word, in prayer, through people and circumstances, and by the Holy Spirit. Hearing God's voice requires a willingness to listen, an open heart, and obedience to His guidance. As we listen, God leads us in truth and helps us grow closer to Him.

Real-Life Story

Elisabeth Elliot: Trusting God's Voice in Hard Times Elisabeth Elliot, a missionary and author, faced the tragedy of her husband Jim's death at the hands of the rural Ecuadorian tribe they were trying to reach for Christ. In the midst of loss, she learned to listen to God's voice for comfort, guidance, and purpose. Later, in obedience to the Lord's direction, she returned to that same tribe to share the gospel, forgiving those who had killed her husband. Her act of forgiveness and obedience led to the eventual healing and transformation of the whole tribe. Elisabeth's story teaches us that listening to

God isn't always easy, but His voice leads us to healing, forgiveness, and hope (Elliot, 1989, *Shadow of the Almighty*).

Prayer

"God, help me to hear Your voice clearly in all areas of my life. Open my heart to receive Your guidance through Your Word, in prayer, and by the Holy Spirit. Give me the courage to listen and obey, trusting that Your ways are best. Amen."

THE BIBLE – GOD'S WORD

Practical Challenge

Choose one verse this week to memorize and reflect on. Write it down, carry it with you, and repeat it throughout the day. Ask God to help you apply that verse in specific situations that arise.

Day 1: Why the Bible is Relevant Today

Scripture: *Hebrews 4:12* - "For the word of God is alive and powerful. It is sharper than the sharpest two-edged sword, cutting between soul and spirit, between joint and marrow. It exposes our innermost thoughts and desires." (NLT)

Reflection: The Bible isn't just an old book — it's alive and active, speaking into our lives today. God's Word has the power to change our hearts, convict us of sin, and guide our paths. No matter how much the world changes, the truths in the Bible remain timeless and relevant for every situation we face.

Journal Question: How has reading the Bible impacted your understanding of God? Your understanding of yourself? Your understanding of the world?

Day 2: Understanding the Bible's Structure (Old and New Testament)

Scripture: *Luke 24:44* - "He said to them, 'This is what I told you while I was still with you: Everything must be fulfilled that is written about me in the Law of Moses, the Prophets and the Psalms.'" (NIV)

Reflection: The Bible is made up of two main sections — the Old Testament and the New Testament. The Old Testament contains the history, law, and prophecies leading up to Jesus. The New Testament focuses on the life of Jesus, the early church, and teachings for believers. Though the Old and New Testament can seem very different, they actually work together to reveal God's story of redemption and His plan for the world from the beginning of time to the end of time. They present one continuous story of God working to restore people to unity with Himself.

Journal Question: Which parts of the Bible do you find most challenging to understand or apply to your life? Does thinking of the entire Bible as one big, connected story of God's redemption help your understanding?

Day 3: How to Read and Study the Bible Effectively

Scripture: *2 Timothy 2:15* - "Do your best to present yourself to God as one approved, a worker who does not need to be ashamed and who correctly handles the word of truth." (NIV)

Reflection: Reading the Bible should be more than just skimming words on a page. Studying it involves learning the context, meditating on its meaning, and asking God to reveal how it applies to your life. One helpful method for starting a practice of studying the Bible is to start with a book like John or Proverbs and read a small section each day, praying for God to speak to you through His Word. Then listen for any connections the Holy Spirit might bring to your mind. It could be connections to other passages of Scripture, connections to experiences in your life, or connections to something you heard or read elsewhere that helps bring out the meaning and relevance of what you're reading.

Journal Question: What strategies have you found that help you study the Bible more effectively? Are there any new strategies that you would like to try to aid your study of Scripture?

Day 4: The Importance of Memorizing Scripture

Scripture: *Psalm 119:11* - "I have hidden your word in my heart, that I might not sin against you." (NLT)

Reflection: Memorizing scripture helps us carry God's truth with us wherever we go. When we are faced with temptation, discouragement, or decisions, having God's Word in our hearts gives us strength and guidance. Start by memorizing simple verses that encourage you and build from there.

Journal Question: How has memorizing scripture been helpful to you in facing challenges?

Day 5: Applying God's Word in Daily Life

Scripture: *Luke 11:28* - "Jesus replied, 'But even more blessed are all who hear the word of God and put it into practice.'" (NLT)

Reflection: Reading and memorizing the Bible are only part of the journey; we must also apply it to our lives. God's Word is meant to be lived out — in how we speak, act, and treat others. Ask the Lord each day how you can apply what you've read, and look for opportunities to put God's Word into action.

Journal Question: What is one way you can apply what you've read from the Bible in your daily life?

Weekly Summary

This week, we discovered why the Bible is still relevant today, learned about the Bible's structure, and explored how to read, study, memorize, and apply it. God's Word is not just a book to be read — it's a living guide meant to shape our lives and draw us closer to God. The more we engage with the Bible, the more we see God's truth and His plan for us and the world.

Real-Life Story

Dietrich Bonhoeffer: Grounded in the Word of God Dietrich Bonhoeffer was a German pastor and theologian who stood against the Nazi regime during World War II. While in prison for his faith and opposition to Hitler's regime, he spent hours reading and meditating on the Bible. Even as he awaited his impending execution, Bonhoeffer found strength, courage, and hope through God's Word. In the darkest times, he remained grounded in biblical truth, and throughout his time in prison, he wrote letters to his friends, encouraging them in the Gospel and in God's faithfulness. The letters he wrote while in prison were published by a friend of his after Bonhoeffer's execution in a work titled *Letters and Papers from Prison*. Those letters continue to be an encouragement to believers today, long after Bonhoeffer's death. Bonhoeffer's story shows us that being deeply rooted in God's word can strengthen us to face even the gravest challenges (Metaxas, 2010).

Prayer

"God, thank You for giving me Your Word. Help me to read, understand, and apply the Bible to my life. Give me a desire to know You more through Scripture, and let Your Word guide my steps each day. Help me to live out my faith boldly because of the truth of Your Word. Amen."

WEEK 8

THE POWER OF WORSHIP

Practical Challenge

Choose one new way to worship God this week. Whether it's through singing, serving someone in need, or taking time to thank God for His blessings, find a creative way to express your worship and draw closer to Him.

Day 1: Worship as a Response to God's Greatness

Scripture: *Psalm 95:6* - "Oh come, let us worship and bow down; let us kneel before the Lord our Maker." (NKJV)

Reflection: Worship is our response to who God is. It's not just singing songs but an attitude of the heart that honors God for His greatness, power, and love. When we worship, we recognize how big God is and how worthy He is of our praise, adoration, and gratitude.

Journal Question: In what area of your life can you honor God more intentionally as an act of worship?

Day 2: Different Forms of Worship (Singing, Serving, Living)

Scripture: *Colossians 3:17* - "And whatever you do or say, do it as a representative of the Lord Jesus, giving thanks through him to God the Father." (NLT)

Reflection: Worship comes in many forms — singing praises to God, serving others, or even doing your daily work with a heart of gratitude. True worship is a lifestyle, not limited to church services. Every action can be an act of worship when it's done with a heart that honors God.

Journal Question: What are some different ways you can worship God throughout the week?

Day 3: Why Worship Connects Us Deeply with God

Scripture: *Psalm 22:3* - "But You *are* holy, enthroned in the praises of Israel." (NKJV)

Reflection: Worship brings us closer to God. When we praise Him, we shift our focus from our problems to His greatness. Worship invites God's presence into our lives and helps us experience His peace, joy, and strength in fresh ways. Worship connects our hearts to God's and deepens our relationship with Him.

Journal Question: How have you seen worship help you connect more deeply with God?

Day 4: Worshiping in Spirit and Truth

Scripture: *John 4:24* - "God *is* Spirit, and those who worship Him must worship in spirit and truth." (NKJV)

Reflection: True worship is about more than just going through the motions; it comes from a sincere heart and a genuine connection to God's truth. Worshiping "in spirit and in truth" means allowing the Holy Spirit to guide our worship and being honest before God. It's about authenticity, not just routines.

Journal Question: What does it mean to you to worship in "spirit and truth"?

Day 5: Worship as a Lifestyle, Not Just an Event

Scripture: *Romans 12:1* - "And so, dear brothers and sisters, I plead with you to give your bodies to God because of all he has done for you. Let them be a living and holy sacrifice—the kind he will find acceptable. This is truly the way to worship him." (NLT)

Reflection: Worship isn't just something we do on Sundays — it's how we live every day. Offering our lives as "living sacrifices" means honoring God in our thoughts, actions, and decisions. When we see our entire lives as an act of worship, everything we do becomes an opportunity to glorify God.

Journal Question: How can you make worship a part of your daily life, not just a Sunday activity?

Weekly Summary

This week, we learned that worship is more than just singing; it's a response to God's greatness, a way to connect with Him, and a lifestyle of honoring Him in all we do. Worshiping in spirit and truth helps us live authentically for God. When we worship with our whole lives, we invite God's presence into every moment and draw closer to Him.

Real-Life Story

Matt Redman: Heart of Worship Matt Redman, a Christian worship leader and songwriter, learned the power of worship through a season where his church stripped away all musical instruments and sound systems to focus purely on worshiping God from the heart. Out of that experience, he wrote the well-known song, "The Heart of Worship." The song's lyrics remind us that worship is not about performance or appearance — it's about bringing our hearts sincerely before God (ACS International, n.d.). Reflecting on this season of his life, Matt once said, "In the end, worship can never be a performance, something you're pretending or putting on. It's got to be an overflow of your heart...Worship is about getting personal with God, drawing close to God" (Redman, 2002). True worship is about connecting with God and honoring Him with everything we are.

Prayer

"God, help me to see worship as more than just songs, but as a way of living for You. Let my life be a reflection of Your greatness and help me to worship in spirit and in truth. Teach me how to draw closer to You through worship each day. Amen."

WEEK 9

FAITH IN ACTION

Practical Challenge

Do one intentional act of kindness each day this week. It can be as simple as sharing a kind word, doing a helpful deed, or listening to someone who needs to share what's on their heart. Let your actions be a reflection of your faith and love for God.

Day 1: Living Out Your Faith Through Words and Actions

Scripture: *James 2:17* - "Thus also faith by itself, if it does not have works, is dead." (NKJV)

Reflection: Faith isn't just something we believe — it's something we live out. Real faith is seen in how we speak, act, and treat others. When we live out our faith through love, kindness, and obedience to God, we show the world who Jesus is and why He is worth following.

Journal Question: How can your words and actions reflect your faith today?

Day 2: Examples of Faith in Action from the Bible

Scripture: *Hebrews 11:1* - "Faith shows the reality of what we hope for; it is the evidence of things we cannot see." (NLT)

Reflection: The Bible is full of stories of people who put their faith into action — from Noah building an ark to Abraham leaving his home to follow God's promise. These "heroes of faith" inspire us to trust God even when we can't see the full picture. Like them, we are called to take bold steps of faith and trust God's plan for our lives.

Journal Question: Who in the Bible inspires you to live out your faith boldly? Why?

Day 3: How Small Acts of Kindness Reflect Our Faith

Scripture: *Galatians 6:10* - "Therefore, whenever we have the opportunity, we should do good to everyone—especially to those in the family of faith." (NLT)

Reflection: Living out our faith doesn't always mean doing big things; it can start with small acts of kindness. Helping a friend, encouraging someone who's down, or standing up for what's right are acts of faith that show God's love. These fruits of the Spirit reflect our faith and allow others to see God's character through us.

Journal Question: What small acts of kindness can you do to show God's love to others? Have you ever experienced God's love through an act of kindness that was done toward you?

Day 4: The Importance of Consistency in Living Out Your Beliefs

Scripture: *Philippians 4:9* - "Keep putting into practice all you learned and received from me—everything you heard from me and saw me doing. Then the God of peace will be with you." (NLT)

Reflection: Living out your faith isn't a one-time thing — it's about consistency. People are watching how you live, and your example can make a difference. Even as a young person, you can be a strong example of faith by staying true to what you believe in both good times and bad. Of course, this doesn't mean you won't ever make mistakes, but even taking steps to ask forgiveness or repent of sin are powerful demonstrations of faith that set an example for people around you.

Journal Question: In what areas of your life do you want to be more consistent in living out your faith?

Day 5: Trusting God to Use Your Faith to Impact Others

Scripture: *Matthew 5:16* - "Let your light so shine before men, that they may see your good works and glorify your Father in heaven." (NKJV)

Reflection: When you live out your faith, you become a light to others. Trust that God can use your actions and words to draw others closer to Him. It's not about being perfect but about letting God's love come out in every area of your life, even in areas where you need repentance and forgiveness. Let your life be a testimony that points others to Jesus and His healing and redemption.

Journal Question: How can you make yourself available for God to use your words and actions to impact others this week?

Weekly Summary

This week, we explored how our faith isn't just a belief but a lifestyle. Faith in action means living out our beliefs through words, actions, kindness, and consistency. Our daily choices and how we treat others reflect God's character and have the power to impact the world around us.

Real-Life Story

William Booth: Faith in Action Through Service William Booth, the founder of The Salvation Army, devoted his life to living out his faith by serving the poor, homeless, and needy. Booth believed that faith should be active and make a tangible difference in the lives of others. He famously said, "Faith and works should travel side by side, step answering to step, like the legs of men walking. First faith, and then works; and then faith again, and then works again — until they can scarcely distinguish which is the one and which is the other" (Booth, 1890). Booth's life teaches us that our faith should be more than words; it should lead to action that reflects God's love to those around us.

Prayer

"Lord, help me to live out my faith through my words and actions. Let my life be a light that reflects Your love and points others to You. Give me the courage to show radical kindness and to be consistent in my walk with You each day. Amen."

TRUSTING GOD IN DIFFICULT TIMES

Practical Challenge

Identify a current struggle or challenge you are facing. Spend time each day praying about it, reading scripture related to trust, and speaking words of hope over your situation. Ask God to help you trust Him more deeply in that area.

Day 1: God is Present Even When Life is Hard

Scripture: *Psalm 46:1* - "God *is* our refuge and strength, a very present help in trouble." (NKJV)

Reflection: Life can be tough, and there are times when we face struggles, pain, and confusion. But God promises to be with us in those moments. He is our refuge — a place of safety and comfort. Even when things don't make sense, God is near, ready to provide strength and peace.

Journal Question: When facing difficult times, how do you usually respond? How can you grow in trusting God during those times?

Day 2: Stories of People Who Trusted God Through Trials

Scripture: *Job 1:21* - "He said,'I came naked from my mother's womb, and I will be naked when I leave. The Lord gave me what I had, and the Lord has taken it away. Praise the name of the Lord!'" (NLT)

Reflection: Job faced immense suffering — losing his family, wealth, and personal health all within a very short timeframe. Despite all this, he chose to trust God. He didn't understand why he was going through such trials, but he held onto his faith and chose to trust God anyway. Job's story reminds us that we can trust God even when life is hard, knowing that He is still in control and working for our good.

Journal Question: What lessons can you learn from the story of Job and how he handled suffering? Are there any ways you feel like you can personally relate to Job's story?

Day 3: How Difficulties Can Strengthen Your Faith

Scripture: *James 1:2-3* - "My brethren, count it all joy when you fall into various trials, knowing that the testing of your faith produces patience." (NKJV)

Reflection: Challenges are an opportunity for growth. While it may seem strange to find joy in hard times, these struggles test and strengthen your faith. God uses difficult circumstances to build character, develop perseverance, and draw you closer to Him. Trust that He is shaping you through every challenge and find joy in being sure that His goodness is at work in your life in every season.

Journal Question: How have challenges in your life strengthened your faith?

Day 4: The Importance of Holding Onto Hope

Scripture: *Romans 15:13* - "May the God of hope fill you with all joy and peace as you trust in him, so that you may overflow with hope by the power of the Holy Spirit." (NIV)

Reflection: In the middle of difficult times, hope anchors our faith. When we trust in God's promises, He fills us with joy and peace that go beyond our circumstances. This hope is not wishful thinking but a confident expectation rooted in God's faithfulness and love. God's unchanging character is our source of hope. Hold onto this hope, knowing that God is with you.

Journal Question: What promises of God give you hope in hard times?

Day 5: Practical Ways to Trust God During Struggles

Scripture: *1 Samuel 14:6* - "'Let's go across to the outpost of those pagans,' Jonathan said to his armor bearer. 'Perhaps the Lord will help us, for nothing can hinder the Lord. He can win a battle whether he has many warriors or only a few!'" (NLT)

Reflection: Trusting God in difficult times doesn't come naturally, but there are practical ways to grow in trust: pray about your struggles, remember God's past faithfulness, and lean on supportive friends or mentors. Remember that God is not surprised by your circumstances, and He had a plan in place for this moment before you were even born. God isn't limited by whatever resources you see available to you in the moment of your struggle. Most importantly, submit your fears and questions to God every time they surface again, knowing that He is guiding you and working things out for your good.

Journal Question: What is one practical step you can take to trust God more deeply in the middle of your struggles?

Weekly Summary

This week was about learning to trust God when life is hard. We explored how God is present in our struggles, how trials can strengthen our faith, and how to hold onto hope. Trusting God doesn't mean understanding everything, but it means relying on His presence, love, and promises no matter what we face.

Real-Life Story

Joni Eareckson Tada: Finding Hope Amidst Suffering Joni Eareckson Tada became a quadriplegic after a diving accident at the age of 17. Instead of allowing her suffering to consume her, she trusted God in the midst of her struggles. Joni learned to paint using her mouth, wrote books, and started a ministry to help others with disabilities. Reflecting back on her journey at one point, she said, "God's greatest blessings come through most unlikely and unexpected places, through pain and suffering" (Tada, 2010).

Her story is a testament to how God can use our pain for a greater purpose and how trust in Him can lead to hope and joy even in the hardest of times.

Prayer

"Dear God, help me to trust You more in the difficult times. Remind me that You are always with me and that You are working all things together for my good. Fill my heart with hope and help me to rely on Your strength and presence each day. Amen."

WEEK 11

GOD'S PLAN FOR MY LIFE

Practical Challenge

Choose one decision you are facing and ask God to guide you in it. Spend time praying, reading Scripture, and listening for His direction. Trust that He will show you the next step, even if it's small.

Day 1: Understanding That God Has a Unique Plan for Each Person

Scripture: *Jeremiah 29:11* - " For I know the thoughts that I think toward you, says the Lord, thoughts of peace and not of evil, to give you a future and a hope." (NKJV)

Reflection: God has a unique plan for each one of us — a plan that is good, full of hope, and purposeful. He created you with special gifts, talents, and dreams that He wants you to use for His glory. If you come to the place of embracing that God's plan is not just general but specific to you, you can engage your life with confident expectation.

Journal Question: How would believing God has a unique plan for you change the way you approach your life?

Day 2: Learning to Seek God's Direction Through Prayer and Scripture

Scripture: *Psalm 32:8* - "I will instruct you and teach you in the way you should go; I will counsel you with my loving eye on you." (NIV)

Reflection: God desires to guide you through every decision and step in life. He promises to instruct and teach you as you seek Him. Prayer and reading Scripture are two powerful ways to hear God's voice and discover His direction for your life. He wants to lead you on the right path — you just have to ask and listen.

Journal Question: What steps can you take to seek God's direction through prayer and reading His Word?

Day 3: Patience in Waiting for God's Timing

Scripture: *Psalm 27:14* - "Wait on the Lord; be of good courage, and He shall strengthen your heart; wait, I say, on the Lord!" (NKJV)

Reflection: God's plan unfolds over time, and waiting can be hard. But God's timing is perfect. He knows what's best and when to bring things into your life. Patience while waiting on God's timing builds trust and maturity. Instead of rushing ahead to make things happen on your own, choose to rest in God's plan and know that He is working all things together for your good in His perfect time.

Journal Question: In what areas of your life are you struggling to be patient for God's timing?

Day 4: Trusting God Even When His Plan is Unclear

Scripture: *Psalm 37:5* - "Commit everything you do to the Lord. Trust him, and he will help you." (NLT)

Reflection: There will be times when God's plan doesn't make sense or feels unclear. It's in those moments that trust becomes crucial. Leaning on your own understanding can lead to confusion and worry, but when you submit to God, He makes the path clear when it's time for the next step. Trust Him to guide your steps, even when you can't see the full picture.

Journal Question: Where in your life can you choose to trust God right now, even though you don't understand His plan?

Day 5: Taking Small Steps of Obedience Toward God's Calling

Scripture: *Micah 6:8* - "No, O people, the Lord has told you what is good, and this is what he requires of you: to do what is right, to love mercy, and to walk humbly with your God." (NLT)

Reflection: God's plan for your life often starts with small steps of obedience. Walking humbly with God means listening to His voice and following His lead, one step at a time. You don't have to know the whole plan to begin walking in obedience — just be willing to trust and take the next step He shows you.

Journal Question: What is one small step of obedience you can take toward God's calling this week?

Weekly Summary

This week, we explored how God has a unique plan for each person and how to seek His direction through prayer and Scripture. We also learned the importance of patience in waiting for God's timing, trusting Him even when His plan is unclear, and taking small steps of obedience. Remember, God has a purpose for your life, and He will guide you one step at a time as you seek Him.

Real-Life Story

Hudson Taylor: Trusting God's Plan in Missions Hudson Taylor was a pioneering British missionary to China in the 1800s, a time in history when travel to China - especially inland China - was very difficult and dangerous. Keeping contact with the outside world and raising support from outside the country were nearly impossible. Taylor embraced his mission anyway, knowing that God had called him to inland China, and he ended up founding the China Inland Mission and brought the gospel to many who had never heard it.

One memorable story about Hudson Taylor involves his decision to adopt Chinese dress and shave his head in the style of Chinese men—a bold move that shocked many of his fellow missionaries and friends. Taylor felt strongly that he needed to identify with the local people to effectively share the gospel. This decision included wearing traditional Chinese clothing, which many Western missionaries found unnecessary and even undignified. Taylor's choice baffled those close to him; they thought he was going too far and didn't understand why he would abandon his own culture so completely. Yet, to Taylor, this was a step of faith and cultural respect. He believed that by dressing and living as the Chinese did, he could better connect with them and share the gospel in a way they could embrace. This approach later became a foundational practice in missions, emphasizing respect for local culture and adaptability. Taylor's trust in God's plan and willingness to obey, even when the path was unclear or didn't make sense, serve as inspiration for us to follow God wherever He leads (Taylor, 1997).

Prayer

"Lord, thank You for having a unique plan for my life. Help me to seek Your direction through prayer and Your Word. Give me patience to wait for Your timing and trust You even when I don't understand. Help me to take small steps of obedience toward the calling You have for me each day. Amen."

WEEK 12

OBEYING GOD

Practical Challenge

Identify one area in your life where you have struggled to obey God. Make a commitment to take one step of obedience this week, trusting that God will bless and strengthen you as you follow Him.

Day 1: What Obedience Looks Like in Everyday Life

Scripture: *John 14:15* - "If you love Me, keep My commandments." (NKJV)

Reflection: Obeying God is not just about the big decisions; it's also about the small choices we make every day. From how we speak to others to how we spend our time, every decision is an opportunity to honor God. Obedience is a way to show our love for Him and to walk in His will.

Journal Question: What are some small ways you can obey God in your daily life?

Day 2: The Blessings That Come from Obedience

Scripture: *Deuteronomy 28:1-2* - "If you fully obey the Lord your God and carefully keep all his commands that I am giving you today, the Lord your God will set you high above all the nations of the world. You will experience all these blessings if you obey the Lord your God:" (NLT)

Reflection: God promises blessings to those who obey Him. These blessings may not always be material, but they include peace, joy, and a deeper relationship with God. Obedience aligns your life with God's best for you, allowing you to experience His favor and presence in a powerful way.

Journal Question: How have you experienced God's blessings as a result of obedience?

Day 3: Examples of Obedience in the Bible

Scripture: *Genesis 12:1-2* - "Now the Lord had said to Abram: 'Get out of your country, from your family and from your father's house, to a land that I will show you. I will make you a great nation; I will bless you and make your name great; and you shall be a blessing.'" (NKJV)

Reflection: Abraham's obedience to God's call led him to leave his home and go to an unknown land. Despite uncertainty about where exactly God was leading him, Abraham trusted God's promise and obeyed. Abraham's willingness to obey God's invitation was the beginning of God setting apart an entire nation of people to demonstrate His character to the world and to eventually bring about the birth of the promised Savior – Jesus. Abraham's story shows us that obedience often requires faith and courage. When we step out in obedience, God uses our actions to fulfill His greater plan.

Journal Question: What do you learn from Abraham's example of obedience, and how can you apply it to your life?

Day 4: Overcoming Challenges That Make Obedience Difficult

Scripture: *Galatians 5:16* - "So I say, let the Holy Spirit guide your lives. Then you won't be doing what your sinful nature craves." (NLT)

Reflection: Obedience is not always easy. Temptations, fear, and distractions can make it hard to follow God's commands. But God gives us the Holy Spirit to help us overcome these challenges. When we walk with the Holy Spirit, we find strength to obey even when it's tough. Ask the Holy Spirit to guide you and empower you to walk in obedience.

Journal Question: What challenges make it hard for you to obey God? How can you rely on the Holy Spirit to help you?

Day 5: Choosing Obedience Over the Opinions of Others

Scripture: *Acts 5:29* - "But Peter and the apostles replied, 'We must obey God rather than any human authority.'" (NLT)

Reflection: Sometimes, obeying God means going against what others think or expect. The apostles faced persecution for sharing the gospel, but they chose to obey God rather than people. When you are faced with the choice between following God's way or pleasing others, remember that obeying God makes the statement that He is the Lord of your life and leads to lasting rewards.

Journal Question: In what situations do you find it difficult to choose obedience to God over the opinions of others? How can you shift your perspective on those situations to line up with God's eternal perspective?

Weekly Summary

This week, we learned what obedience looks like in daily life and the blessings that come from it. We also saw examples of biblical obedience, discovered how to overcome challenges to obedience, and explored choosing God's way over the opinions of others. Obedience isn't just about rules — it's about living a life that honors God and walks in His will.

Real-Life Story

David Wilkerson: A Call to Obedience in Ministry David Wilkerson was an American pastor who felt God calling him to reach out to troubled gang members and drug addicts in New York City in the 1950s. In one notable encounter, Wilkerson approached Nicky Cruz, a notorious gang leader of the feared gang, the Mau Maus. Cruz, who had lived a life filled with violence and anger, threatened Wilkerson and told him he would kill him if he didn't leave. Undeterred, Wilkerson famously responded, "You could cut me into a thousand pieces and lay them in the street, and every piece would still love you."

Wilkerson's courage, faith, and love were disarming. Despite the real danger, he continued to reach out to Cruz and other gang members with God's message of forgiveness and redemption. Over time, his persistence broke through to Cruz, who eventually gave his life to Christ. This encounter marked the beginning of Wilkerson's ministry, Teen Challenge, which went on to help thousands of gang members, drug addicts, and troubled youth find freedom from addiction and hope in Christ. His obedience to God's leading led to countless transformed lives and demonstrates how powerful obedience can be when we listen and respond to God's voice (Wilkerson, 1963).

Prayer

"God, help me to obey You in all areas of my life. Thank You for the blessings that come from obedience. Give me the strength and courage to follow You, even when it's hard, and help me to choose Your way over the opinions of others. Amen."

DEVELOPING SPIRITUAL HABITS

Practical Challenge

Choose one spiritual habit to focus on this week. Whether it's setting aside time to read the Bible, praying daily, worshiping intentionally, fasting for a meal, or finding an accountability partner, make it a goal to be consistent with that habit and see how it helps you grow.

Day 1: The Importance of Daily Bible Reading

Scripture: *Matthew 4:4* - "Jesus answered, 'It is written: "Man shall not live on bread alone, but on every word that comes from the mouth of God."'" (NIV)

Reflection: Just as our bodies need food to stay healthy, our spirits need the nourishment of God's Word. Developing the habit of reading the Bible daily helps us grow in our relationship with God and gives us wisdom and guidance. It is also one of the means by which God renews our minds and cleanses us of the "old man" as a part of His ongoing redemption and sanctification at work in our lives. Make time each day to meditate on Scripture, allowing it to shape your thoughts and actions.

Journal Question: What spiritual habits do you currently have, and how do they help you grow closer to God? Which spiritual habits do you think you need to improve on?

Day 2: Setting Aside Time for Solitude and Silence

Scripture: *Mark 1:35* - "Now in the morning, having risen a long while before daylight, He went out and departed to a solitary place; and there He prayed." (NKJV)

Reflection: Jesus made solitude and silence a priority, often going to a quiet place to connect with God. Setting aside intentional time for prayer and reflection, away from noise and distraction, allows us to deepen our relationship with God, hear His voice, and lay our burdens before Him. It's a time to grow closer to the One who loves us most and be renewed in strength and peace.

Journal Question: What steps can you take to find solitude and silence? Plan a place and date and start your time meditating on Psalm 46:10.

Day 3: Gratitude as a Regular Part of Your Week

Scripture: *Hebrews 13:15* - "Therefore by Him let us continually offer the sacrifice of praise to God, that is, the fruit of *our* lips, giving thanks to His name." (NKJV)

Reflection: Being thankful shifts our perspective. It causes us to remember God's goodness and all that He has done for us and in us. Gratitude helps build our faith to face the circumstances we are in as we recognize God's faithfulness up to this point in our lives. Choosing to be thankful can set us free from negative thoughts and bring us back to a heart of worship.

Journal Question: How has gratitude impacted your perspective of your circumstances and your relationship with God?

Day 4: Fasting and Other Spiritual Disciplines

Scripture: *Matthew 6:17-18* - "But when you fast, comb your hair and wash your face. Then no one will notice that you are fasting, except your Father, who knows what you do in private. And your Father, who sees everything, will reward you." (NLT)

Reflection: Fasting is a spiritual discipline where we give up something — usually food — to focus more on God. It's about seeking God with intensity and dedicating time to prayer. It also serves as a tangible practice of dying to our flesh and its desires and living by the leading of the Spirit.

Journal Question: Reflect on a time where you intentionally gave something up for the sake of obeying the Lord or seeking Him more fully. What fruit did you see out of that decision? If you have not done that before, make a plan to try it for the first time this week.

Day 5: Developing Accountability in Your Spiritual Walk

Scripture: *Ecclesiastes 4:9-10* - "Two people are better off than one, for they can help each other succeed. If one person falls, the other can reach out and help. But someone who falls alone is in real trouble." (NLT)

Reflection: Accountability is a powerful tool in developing spiritual habits. Having someone to encourage you, pray for you, and challenge you to grow keeps you on track in your faith. Find a friend, mentor, or small group who can walk alongside you as you seek to develop habits that honor God.

Journal Question: Who can you ask to be an accountability partner in your spiritual journey? What will you ask them to keep you accountable for?

Weekly Summary

This week, we explored the importance of developing spiritual habits like Bible reading, solitude, gratitude, fasting, and accountability. These practices help us draw closer to God, grow in our faith, and stay grounded in His truth. Cultivating spiritual habits makes our relationship with God deeper and more vibrant.

Real-Life Story

Billy Graham: A Life of Spiritual Discipline Billy Graham, one of the most well-known evangelists in history, was known for his commitment to spiritual habits. He read the Bible daily, spent intentional time in prayer, and prioritized sharing his faith. His disciplined spiritual life enabled him to impact millions of people worldwide with the message of Jesus. As he became more and more successful as an evangelist, he never lost sight of his need to practice spiritual disciplines every day in order to keep his focus on the Lord and his heart in the right place. He once said, "If you don't feel close to God, guess who moved? Discipline yourself to find time each day to talk to God, study His Word, and listen for His voice" (Graham, 2006).

Graham's example reminds us that consistent spiritual habits not only grow our faith but also empower us to share God's love with others.

Prayer

"Dear God, help me to develop spiritual habits that draw me closer to You. Give me the discipline to read Your Word, spend time in silence with You, express gratitude, and seek You in new ways. Surround me with people who will encourage and challenge me to grow in my faith. Amen."

Dealing with Doubts

Practical Challenge

Write down one of your current doubts or questions about God or faith.
Spend time praying about it, searching the Bible for answers, and talking to a
trusted friend or mentor. Ask God to strengthen your faith as you seek Him.

Day 1: Doubts are a Normal Part of Faith

Scripture: *Mark 9:24* - "Immediately the father of the child cried out and said
with tears, 'Lord, I believe; help my unbelief!'" (NKJV)

Reflection: Everyone experiences doubts at times — even strong believers.
Doubts don't mean your faith is weak; they are an opportunity to ask questions and seek deeper understanding. Like this father in the Bible who cried
out to Jesus, bring your doubts to God, knowing He is patient and willing to
help you overcome unbelief.

Journal Question: What doubts or questions do you currently have about your faith?

Day 2: How to Seek Answers to Your Questions

Scripture: *Jeremiah 33:3* - "Ask me and I will tell you remarkable secrets you do not know about things to come." (NLT)

Reflection: When you have doubts or questions, don't be afraid to seek answers. Read the Bible, talk to trusted mentors, and pray for God's wisdom. God promises to reveal truth to those who genuinely seek Him. Your questions can lead to a deeper and more genuine understanding of God's character and love.

Journal Question: How can you begin to actively seek answers to your questions through prayer, Scripture, or talking to trusted mentors?

Day 3: Trusting God Even When You Don't Have All the Answers

Scripture: *Isaiah 26:3* - "You will keep in perfect peace all who trust in you, all whose thoughts are fixed on you!" (NLT)

Reflection: There will be times when you don't understand everything about God or why certain things happen. Trusting God doesn't mean you have all the answers, but it means relying on Him even when you don't. Faith involves trusting God's goodness and wisdom, even in the midst of unanswered questions.

Journal Question: In what areas of your life are you finding it hard to trust God? How can you choose to trust Him even without all the answers?

Day 4: Finding Reassurance in God's Promises

Scripture: *Deuteronomy 31:8* - "Do not be afraid or discouraged, for the Lord will personally go ahead of you. He will be with you; he will neither fail you nor abandon you." (NLT)

Reflection: When doubts creep in, find reassurance in God's promises. He promises to be with you, to strengthen you, and to guide you. When you meditate on God's Word, it helps calm your fears and strengthens your faith. Let God's promises be an anchor that holds you steady in times of doubt.

Journal Question: What promises of God give you peace and reassurance during times of doubt?

Day 5: Surrounding Yourself with People Who Encourage Your Faith

Scripture: *Hebrews 12:1* - "Therefore, since we are surrounded by such a huge crowd of witnesses to the life of faith, let us strip off every weight that slows us down, especially the sin that so easily trips us up. And let us run with endurance the race God has set before us." (NLT)

Reflection: Having a community of believers around you is important when you face doubts. Being surrounded by people who encourage, challenge, and build up your faith can help you overcome struggles and stay strong. Don't isolate yourself in times of doubt — seek support from friends who share your faith and point you back to God.

Journal Question: Who are the people in your life who encourage your faith, and how can you reach out to them when you face struggles?

Weekly Summary

This week, we learned that doubts are a normal part of faith and can lead to deeper understanding when we seek God's answers. Trusting God, even without all the answers, is a step of faith. We also find reassurance in God's promises and strength from the support of fellow believers. Doubts don't have to weaken your faith — they can lead you to a stronger relationship with God.

Real-Life Story

C.S. Lewis: From Atheism to Faith C.S. Lewis, the famous author of *The Chronicles of Narnia*, was once an atheist who had many doubts about God and Christianity. However, he also highly valued truth and sought it out fervently. For a long time, he devoted himself to intense study and research in an effort to prove once-and-for-all that Christianity could not be true. In recalling the culmination of all his research and efforts, Lewis says:

"You must picture me alone in that room in Magdalen, night after night, feeling, whenever my mind lifted even for a second from my work, the steady, unrelenting approach of Him whom I so earnestly desired not to meet. That which I greatly feared had at last come upon me. I gave in, and admitted that God was God, and knelt and prayed: perhaps, that night, the most dejected and reluctant convert in all England" (Lewis, 1955).

Lewis struggled deeply with doubts and resisted belief in God for many years. However, his relentless search for truth eventually led him to a place where he could no longer deny God's presence, marking the beginning of his Christian journey. Through seeking truth, reading Scripture, and talking with friends like J.R.R. Tolkien, Lewis eventually came not only to believe in God, but also to be a strong defender of the Christian faith. His journey shows that doubts can lead to deeper faith when we seek the Truth with open hearts and minds.

Prayer

"God, thank You for being patient with my doubts and questions. Help me to seek You honestly and to find answers that draw me closer to You. Give me the faith to trust You even when I don't have all the answers, and surround me with people who encourage me to grow in my relationship with You. Amen."

THE ROLE OF THE HOLY SPIRIT

Practical Challenge

Pray each day this week for the Holy Spirit to fill and guide you. Spend a few moments asking God to help you grow in the fruits of the Spirit and to rely on His strength in all that you do. Watch how God's Spirit works in your heart and actions.

Day 1: Who the Holy Spirit Is

Scripture: *John 14:26* - "But the Helper, the Holy Spirit, whom the Father will send in My name, He will teach you all things, and bring to your remembrance all things that I said to you." (NKJV)

Reflection: The Holy Spirit is God's presence living within us. Jesus promised the Holy Spirit as a helper, teacher, and guide to believers. Understanding who the Holy Spirit is helps us see that we are not alone in our walk with God. He gives us wisdom, comfort, and strength to live out our faith every day.

Journal Question: In what ways have you seen the Holy Spirit at work in your life so far? In what ways would you like to experience more of the Holy Spirit's activity in your life?

Day 2: How the Holy Spirit Guides and Comforts Us

Scripture: *Romans 8:14* - "For as many as are led by the Spirit of God, these are sons of God." (NKJV)

Reflection: The Holy Spirit actively guides us in our decisions, thoughts, and actions. We just have to take the time to pay attention. When we are feeling lost, discouraged, or uncertain, the Holy Spirit brings comfort and direction. He speaks to our hearts, leading us closer to God's will for our lives. Ask the Holy Spirit to guide you and be open to His leading in every situation. Take time in silence and create space to really hear what the Holy Spirit is saying to your spirit.

Journal Question: In what ways has the Holy Spirit guided or comforted you recently? Are there any areas of your life where you might need to slow down so that you can pay attention to where the Holy Spirit is guiding you?

Day 3: The Fruits of the Spirit

Scripture: *Galatians 5:22-23* - "But the fruit of the Spirit is love, joy, peace, longsuffering, kindness, goodness, faithfulness, gentleness, self-control. Against such there is no law." (NKJV)

Reflection: When we live by the Holy Spirit's guidance, our lives produce "fruit" that reflects God's character. These fruits — love, joy, peace, patience, kindness, goodness, faithfulness, gentleness, and self-control — show the world Jesus' character. Growing in these areas is a sign that the Holy Spirit is actively at work in your life.

Journal Question: Which fruit of the Spirit do you feel God wants to grow in you more at this time in your life? Why?

Day 4: How to Be Filled with the Holy Spirit

Scripture: *Ephesians 5:18* - "Don't be drunk with wine, because that will ruin your life. Instead, be filled with the Holy Spirit," (NLT)

Reflection: Being filled with the Holy Spirit is a gift that Jesus told his disciples to wait for after His ascension because He knew it was so essential to living out a life of godliness. Just as a car needs fuel to run, we need the Holy Spirit to live out our faith effectively. If you aren't sure whether you have received Jesus' gift of the Holy Spirit, pray for the Holy Spirit to fill your life, guide your thoughts, and empower your actions. Surrendering to the Spirit allows God to work powerfully through you.

Journal Question: Is the Holy Spirit the fuel that you run on? If not, what is? What steps of surrender and repentance do you need to take to step under the Holy Spirit's leadership?

Day 5: Relying on the Holy Spirit for Daily Strength

Scripture: *Zechariah 4:6* - "So he answered and said to me: 'This *is* the word of the Lord to Zerubbabel: "Not by might nor by power, but by My Spirit," Says the Lord of hosts."' (NKJV)

Reflection: Our own strength and abilities can only take us so far. To embrace our high calling in Christ Jesus and overcome the challenges that will try to keep us from living into our full identity as children of God, we need the power of the Holy Spirit. Each day, rely on the Holy Spirit to give you the strength, wisdom, and courage you need to face whatever comes your way. Trust that God's Spirit will empower you to live victoriously.

Journal Question: Where do you need to see the Holy Spirit's empowering grace and strength at work in your life right now? Is there anything you have been trying to accomplish in your own strength that you can hand over to the Holy Spirit?

Weekly Summary

This week, we learned about the role of the Holy Spirit as our guide, teacher, and source of strength. The Holy Spirit produces fruit in our lives, and being filled with the Spirit empowers us to live in a way that honors God. Relying on the Holy Spirit daily helps us grow in our faith and equips us to navigate life's challenges and live into our identities as Gods' children.

Real-Life Story

Smith Wigglesworth: A Life Transformed by the Holy Spirit Smith Wigglesworth, a British evangelist in the early 20th century, was known for his passionate faith and reliance on the Holy Spirit. But he wasn't always confident in his faith. His early life was marked by his focus on his career as a plumber, periods of struggling with doubt, and a lack of desire to grow in his faith. But when he accepted a friend's invitation to a meeting where an evangelist was preaching, he was stirred with a strong desire to have a deeper relationship with the Lord. He requested prayer to be baptized in the Holy Spirit, and his life was transformed. He began preaching, praying for miraculous healings for others, and boldly sharing the Gospel around the world. The Holy Spirit empowers ordinary people to do extraordinary things for God (Wigglesworth, 2002).

Prayer

"Lord, thank You for sending the Holy Spirit to live within me. Help me to understand the Spirit's role in my life and to rely on the Spirit's guidance and strength daily. Fill me with more of Your Spirit so that I may live a life that honors You, and empower me to show the world who You are by the fruit of Your Spirit at work in me. Amen."

WEEK 16

GOD'S GRACE AND FORGIVENESS

Practical Challenge

Take time this week to reflect on God's grace and forgiveness. If there is an area where you need to forgive yourself or someone else, ask God to help you take that step. Write down a verse about grace to carry with you and remind yourself of God's unconditional love and forgiveness.

Day 1: Understanding Grace as a Gift from God

Scripture: *Ephesians 2:8-9* - "God saved you by his grace when you believed. And you can't take credit for this; it is a gift from God. Salvation is not a reward for the good things we have done, so none of us can boast about it." (NLT)

Reflection: Grace is God's unearned favor toward us. It's a gift that we cannot work for or deserve, and it is through grace that we are saved. Understanding grace helps us see that God's love for us is not based on our performance but on His mercy. Accepting this grace has the power to change the way we see ourselves and how we relate to God.

Journal Question: What does grace mean to you, and how have you experienced God's grace in your life?

Day 2: Why We Need God's Forgiveness

Scripture: *Romans 3:23-24* - "For everyone has sinned; we all fall short of God's glorious standard. Yet God, in his grace, freely makes us right in his sight. He did this through Christ Jesus when he freed us from the penalty for our sins." (NLT)

Reflection: Every person has sinned and fallen short of God's perfect standard. Sin separates us from God and His holiness, but God's forgiveness through Jesus' sacrifice bridges that gap. We need God's forgiveness to be able to come into a relationship with Him. When we confess our sins, God is faithful to forgive and cleanse us, making it possible for us to come into close relationship with Him again.

Journal Question: How does understanding God's grace change the way you see yourself and others?

Day 3: How to Accept God's Grace and Forgive Ourselves

Scripture: *1 John 1:9* - "If we confess our sins, He is faithful and just to forgive us *our* sins and to cleanse us from all unrighteousness." (NKJV)

Reflection: Accepting God's grace means confessing our sins and trusting that He has forgiven us. But sometimes, even after God forgives us, we struggle to forgive ourselves. Remember that God's grace is bigger than any mistake or failure. Practicing forgiving ourselves when God has forgiven us is one of the ways that we acknowledge God's leadership in our lives. If He says that our mistake is taken care of, it is not our place to say that we don't deserve forgiveness or that our sin is too big for Jesus' blood to cover. Let go of shame, accept God's forgiveness, and learn to forgive yourself as an act of faith.

Journal Question: Why do you think it's difficult to accept forgiveness and forgive yourself at times?

Day 4: Offering Grace and Forgiveness to Others

Scripture: *Colossians 3:13* - "Make allowance for each other's faults, and forgive anyone who offends you. Remember, the Lord forgave you, so you must forgive others." (NLT)

Reflection: Just as God has extended grace and forgiveness to us, we are called to extend grace and forgiveness to others. Holding onto anger or bitterness does not punish the person who hurt you; it only keeps you from living in personal freedom. When we forgive others, we reflect God's character, showing His love to the world, and we acknowledge God's leadership in our lives by obeying His command to walk in generous forgiveness. It is not always a one-and-done choice. Often forgiveness is a choice we make every day for a long time if we have been greatly wronged. This humility and daily surrender is precious to the Lord. Forgive, just as you have been generously forgiven.

Journal Question: Who is someone you need to extend grace and forgiveness to? How can you take that step?

Day 5: Living in Freedom Because of God's Grace

Scripture: *Romans 8:1* - *"There is* therefore now no condemnation to those who are in Christ Jesus, who do not walk according to the flesh, but according to the Spirit." (NKJV)

Reflection: God's grace not only forgives us but also frees us from condemnation and guilt. Because of Jesus, we are set free to live in God's love without shame or fear. Living in grace means walking in the freedom that comes from knowing we are fully loved, forgiven, and accepted by God. Stepping into the freedom of God's full forgiveness through Jesus is an act of faith. Step into His mercies that are fresh every day!

Journal Question: Where have you been holding onto shame or condemnation in your life? Hand those areas of your life over to Jesus today, and thank Him for the freedom of His forgiveness.

Weekly Summary

This week, we explored the power of God's grace and forgiveness. Grace is a gift from God, given freely to all who believe. Understanding our need for forgiveness and accepting God's grace allows us to live without shame and offer generous grace to others. God's grace empowers us to walk in freedom and love.

Real-Life Story

John Newton: The Man Behind "Amazing Grace" John Newton's journey to Christianity was as dramatic as it was transformative. Newton, a former slave ship captain, was known for his reckless and profane life. However, one night in 1748, while sailing through a violent storm off the coast of Ireland, he faced what he thought would be certain death. As the storm raged and water flooded the ship, Newton cried out, "Lord, have mercy on us!"

Miraculously, the ship survived, and Newton was left shaken and introspective. That night marked a turning point. Newton began to study the Bible and reflect on his life, eventually embracing Christianity. Over time, his faith grew, and he completely renounced the slave trade, later becoming a pastor and a prominent abolitionist. He would go on to write the famous hymn "Amazing Grace," which beautifully captured his story of redemption: *"I once was lost, but now am found; was blind, but now I see"* (Newton, 2003).

Newton's story reminds us that no matter our past, God's grace is available to all, offering new life and freedom.

Prayer

"God, thank You for Your amazing grace and forgiveness. Help me to accept Your grace fully and to forgive myself as You forgive me. Teach me to extend grace to others and to live in the freedom that comes from being loved and accepted by You. Amen."

EXPERIENCING GOD'S PRESENCE

Practical Challenge

Spend 10 minutes each day this week in quiet reflection or prayer. Turn off distractions and focus on being still before God. Ask Him to reveal His presence to you and to fill your heart with His peace.

Day 1: Recognizing God's Presence in Quiet Moments

Scripture: *Psalm 46:10* - "Be still, and know that I *am* God; I will be exalted among the nations, I will be exalted in the earth!" (NKJV)

Reflection: It's easy to overlook God's presence when life is loud and busy. But God often speaks to us in the quiet moments. Taking time to be still before God allows us to hear His voice and feel His presence. Find a few minutes today to be still and know that God is with you.

Journal Question: When you found time to be still today, what did you feel or hear from the Lord?

Day 2: Feeling God's Presence in Community and Worship

Scripture: *Matthew 18:20* - "For where two or three gather in my name, there am I with them." (NIV)

Reflection: God's presence is not just something we experience alone but also in community. When believers gather for worship, prayer, or fellowship, God's presence is felt in a special way. Worship with others brings joy, encouragement, and the awareness that we are part of God's family. Seek out ways to connect with others and worship together.

Journal Question: How have you experienced God's presence in quiet moments or in worship with others?

Day 3: Trusting That God is With You Even When You Don't Feel Him

Scripture: *Joshua 1:9* - "This is my command—be strong and courageous! Do not be afraid or discouraged. For the Lord your God is with you wherever you go." (NLT)

Reflection: There are times when it may feel like God is far away, but His presence is not based on our feelings. God promises to always be with us, whether we feel His presence or not. Trust in His promise and know that God is always by your side, guiding, protecting, and loving you.

Journal Question: How does trusting that God is *always* present with you affect the way you face difficult times or uncertain situations? How does it affect the way you face the mundane, everyday moments in your life?

Day 4: How to Cultivate a Sense of God's Presence

Scripture: *James 4:8* - "Come close to God, and God will come close to you. Wash your hands, you sinners; purify your hearts, for your loyalty is divided between God and the world." (NLT)

Reflection: Cultivating a sense of God's presence starts with drawing near to Him. Through prayer, worship, reading Scripture, and being mindful of God throughout your day, you can grow more aware of His presence. God desires to be close to you, and as you draw near to Him, He promises to draw near to you.

Journal Question: What are some ways you can draw near to God and become more aware of His presence in your daily life?

Day 5: The Peace That Comes from Knowing God is Always Near

Scripture: *Philippians 4:7* - "Then you will experience God's peace, which exceeds anything we can understand. His peace will guard your hearts and minds as you live in Christ Jesus." (NLT)

Reflection: Experiencing God's presence brings peace that surpasses all understanding. When you know God is near, you can rest in His love and find peace in the middle of life's storms. Let God's presence guard your heart and mind, giving you the calm and assurance that only He can provide.

Journal Question: Where can you see the peace of God at work in your life right now? In what ways can you help others experience God's presence and peace?

Weekly Summary

This week, we learned about experiencing God's presence in quiet moments, in community, and in every season of life. Even when we don't feel God's presence, we can trust that He is always with us. Cultivating an awareness of God's presence brings peace, comfort, and joy as we walk closely with Him.

Real-Life Story

Brother Andrew: Practicing God's Presence in Dangerous Situations
Brother Andrew, also known as "God's Smuggler," risked his life to bring Bibles to Christians in countries where the gospel was forbidden. Even when facing danger, he trusted in God's presence and protection. He would often pray, "Lord, in my luggage I have Scripture that I want to take to Your children. When You were on earth, You made blind eyes see. Now I pray, make seeing eyes blind" (Brother Andrew, 1967).

He has many incredible stories of seeing God intervene in just the right way at just the right moment in his situation so that his life was preserved, and he was able to carry out his mission of bringing the Word of God to isolated believers in closed-off countries. His faith and sense of God's presence with him always empowered him to share God's Word despite the risks.

Prayer

"God, thank You for being near to me. Help me to recognize Your presence in every moment, both in the quiet and in the community of others. Teach me to rest in Your peace and to trust that You are always with me, no matter what I feel. Amen."

WEEK 18

SHARING YOUR FAITH

Practical Challenge

Choose one person this week to intentionally share your faith with.
Whether it's through telling your story, offering to pray for them, or simply
showing kindness, look for an opportunity to reflect God's love and make
Him known.

Day 1: Why Sharing Your Faith is Important

Scripture: *Matthew 28:19* - "Go therefore and make disciples of all the nations, baptizing them in the name of the Father and of the Son and of the
Holy Spirit," (NKJV)

Reflection: Jesus calls all believers to share their faith and make disciples.
Sharing your faith is about letting others know the love and hope you have
found in Jesus. It's not about having all the answers, but about being willing
to tell your story and let God use your story to show His character to others.

Journal Question: Why is sharing your faith important to you personally? If it is not important to you right now, why is that?

Day 2: How to Share Your Testimony with Others

Scripture: *1 Peter 3:15* - "But in your hearts revere Christ as Lord. Always be prepared to give an answer to everyone who asks you to give the reason for the hope that you have. But do this with gentleness and respect," (NIV)

Reflection: Your personal story of how Jesus changed your life and is still working in you is one of the most powerful ways to share your faith. Think about how God has worked in your life and what He is teaching you right now and be ready to share that story with others. Speak from the heart and do so with gentleness and respect, showing the love of Christ in all you say.

Journal Question: How can you prepare to share your testimony with others in a clear and loving way?

Day 3: Overcoming Fear or Nervousness About Evangelism

Scripture: *2 Timothy 1:7* - "For God has not given us a spirit of fear, but of power and of love and of a sound mind." (NKJV)

Reflection: Sharing your faith can feel intimidating, but God's Spirit gives us boldness and courage. You don't need to be perfect or know all the answers to share about Jesus — just be willing to speak up and trust that God will give you the right words. Pray for boldness, and step out in faith to share the gospel with those around you. "Gospel" literally means "good news." The way Jesus has saved you and how He is teaching you, healing you, and encouraging you is good news! It's worth sharing.

Journal Question: What fears or nervousness do you have about sharing your faith? How can you overcome them with Jesus' partnership?

Day 4: Building Relationships Before Sharing Your Faith

Scripture: *Colossians 4:5-6* - "Live wisely among those who are not believers, and make the most of every opportunity. Let your conversation be gracious and attractive so that you will have the right response for everyone." (NLT)

Reflection: Sharing your faith is often more effective when it is done in the context of a genuine relationship. Get to know people, listen to their stories, and truly care about them. When people see your love and kindness, they are more likely to be open to hearing about your faith. Look for opportunities to connect and build friendships, and from that place, point others to Jesus.

Journal Question: Who is someone in your life you can build a relationship with, in order to share your faith more effectively? Who do you already have relationships with that can provide an opportunity for you to share the good news of Jesus?

Day 5: Living a Life That Reflects God's Love to Others

Scripture: *John 13:35* - "By this everyone will know that you are my disciples, if you love one another." (NIV)

Reflection: Sometimes the best way to share your faith is through how you live. When your actions reflect God's love, people take notice. Let your kindness, humility, and joy be a testimony to God's work in your life. Live in a way that shines a light on who Jesus is and demonstrates His extravagant love, making people curious to know more about Him.

Journal Question: What are some ways your actions can reflect God's love and draw others to Him? Have you ever observed how someone else lives and been inspired to know God better because of them? What caught your attention?

Weekly Summary

This week, we explored the importance of sharing our faith and some practical tips for doing it. Sharing your testimony, overcoming fear, building relationships, and living in a way that reflects God's love are all ways to point others to Jesus. Evangelism is not just about what we say but also how we live, and God uses both our words and actions to reach the world around us.

Real-Life Story

Nick Vujicic: Sharing Hope Without Limits Nick Vujicic was born without arms or legs. Because of this, he faced significant challenges in his early life. Growing up, he struggled with feelings of isolation and depression, which led him to contemplate suicide as a teenager. However, during this difficult period, he found new hope and purpose through Jesus. At the age of 15, after reading a Bible verse that spoke to him about his value and purpose, he began to embrace Christianity.

He experienced a profound transformation, realizing that he could use his life to inspire others despite his physical limitations. His newfound faith motivated him to share his story, leading him to become a motivational speaker and author, and eventually, he began traveling around the world to share his story and spread the hope of Jesus. Despite his physical challenges, he uses his life as a testimony of God's love, joy, and purpose. Nick's boldness in sharing his faith inspires countless people to trust God and boldly share their faith, no matter their circumstances (Vujicic, 2010).

Prayer

"Lord, thank You for giving me the opportunity to share Your love with others. Help me to be bold in sharing my faith, to speak from the heart, and to build relationships that point to You. Let my life reflect Your love, and give me courage to be a light to those around me. Amen."

UNDERSTANDING YOUR IDENTITY IN CHRIST

Practical Challenge

Take time this week to memorize a verse that reminds you of your identity in Christ. Write it down, reflect on it, and let it encourage you to live confidently in who God made you to be.

Day 1: What It Means to Be a Child of God

Scripture: *Isaiah 64:8* - "And yet, O Lord, you are our Father. We are the clay, and you are the potter. We all are formed by your hand." (NLT)

Reflection: Your identity is rooted in the fact that you are a child of God, loved and valued by Him. You don't have to earn His love or prove your worth — it's already given to you because of who God is and who He made you to be. Embrace your identity as God's beloved child, and let that truth shape how you see yourself and live your life.

Journal Question: How does knowing you are a child of God change the way you see yourself and your worth?

Day 2: Rejecting the Lies of the World About Your Worth

Scripture: *Romans 12:2* - "Don't copy the behavior and customs of this world, but let God transform you into a new person by changing the way you think. Then you will learn to know God's will for you, which is good and pleasing and perfect." (NLT)

Reflection: The world often tells you lies about who you should be, what makes you valuable, or how you need to look to be accepted. But your worth comes from God, not the world. Reject the lies and let God's truth renew your mind. You are fearfully and wonderfully made, created with purpose, and deeply loved by God.

Journal Question: What lies from the world have you believed about your identity, and how can you replace them with God's truth?

Day 3: Embracing Your Identity as a New Creation in Christ

Scripture: *2 Corinthians 5:17* - "This means that anyone who belongs to Christ has become a new person. The old life is gone; a new life has begun!" (NLT)

Reflection: When you give your life to Jesus, you become a new creation. Your past mistakes, failures, and sins no longer define you — you are made new in Christ. Embrace your identity as someone who is redeemed, forgiven, and transformed by God's love. Live confidently in the freedom and grace that comes from being made new in Him.

Journal Question: What are some ways you can remind yourself daily to live into your God-given identity?

Day 4: How Your Identity Shapes Your Decisions and Actions

Scripture: *Galatians 2:20* - "I have been crucified with Christ; it is no longer I who live, but Christ lives in me; and the *life* which I now live in the flesh I live by faith in the Son of God, who loved me and gave Himself for me." (NKJV)

Reflection: Knowing who you are in Christ shapes the way you live. When you see yourself as God's child, loved and valued by Him, you are more likely to make decisions that honor Him and reflect His character. Let your identity in Christ influence how you speak, act, and treat others. Live in a way that shows the world who God is through your life.

Journal Question: How does your identity as a new creation in Christ shape the way you live and make decisions? Is there any area of your life where you would like to see your identity in Christ expressed more fully than it has been so far?

Day 5: Living Confidently in Who God Says You Are

Scripture: *Psalm 139:13* - "For you created my inmost being; you knit me together in my mother's womb." (NIV)

Reflection: God has known you from the very beginning. He created you intentionally, with purpose and love. Knowing that you were "knit together" by God Himself should give you confidence in your unique design and value. Embrace who God made you to be, and live boldly, knowing that you are deeply loved and wonderfully made.

Journal Question: How can you live more confidently in who God says you are, embracing His purpose for your life?

Weekly Summary

This week, we focused on understanding your identity in Christ. You are a child of God, made new in Him, and created with purpose. Reject the lies of the world, embrace your God-given identity, and let it shape how you live, make decisions, and treat others. Live confidently in who God says you are, and let His truth guide your life.

Real-Life Story

Christine Caine: Living Out Your Identity in Christ Christine Caine faced significant struggles with identity and self-worth during her early life. Growing up in Australia, she dealt with feelings of abandonment, as she was born to an unwed mother and adopted by a family that did not provide a nurturing environment. This led to deep-seated insecurities and a sense of not belonging. Throughout her youth, Christine grappled with issues of self-acceptance and often felt inadequate. However, her life began to change when she encountered the message of God's love for her.

She discovered her identity as a child of God, which became a turning point for her. Through her faith, Christine learned that her worth was not defined by her past experiences or others' opinions, but by her relationship with God. Christine's journey inspired her to share her story with others, and she became a well-known speaker and author, encouraging countless individuals to find their identity in Christ and embrace their worth as beloved children of God. Her message emphasizes the transformative power of God's love in helping us overcome struggles with identity and self-worth (Caine, 2016).

Prayer

"God, thank You for creating me and calling me Your child. Help me to reject the lies of the world and to embrace my identity in You. Let Your truth shape the way I live, and give me confidence to walk boldly in who You say I am. Use my life to reflect Your love and bring glory to You. Amen."

WEEK 20

OVERCOMING INSECURITY

Practical Challenge

Write down three truths about your identity in Christ from Scripture.
When feelings of insecurity come up, read these truths aloud and let them
remind you of your worth in God.

Day 1: Recognizing the Roots of Insecurity

Scripture: *Psalm 139:14* - "I praise you because I am fearfully and wonderfully
made; your works are wonderful, I know that full well." (NIV)

Reflection: Insecurity often comes from focusing on what we think we lack
or comparing ourselves to others. But God's Word reminds you that you are
"fearfully and wonderfully made." God created you with purpose, and He sees
you as valuable and loved. When insecurity arises, remember that your worth
is not determined by what others think — it's rooted in who God says you
are.

Journal Question: What are some insecurities you struggle with, and how can you combat them with God's truth?

Day 2: How to Find Security in God's Love and Approval

Scripture: *Romans 8:38-39* - "And I am convinced that nothing can ever separate us from God's love. Neither death nor life, neither angels nor demons, neither our fears for today nor our worries about tomorrow—not even the powers of hell can separate us from God's love. No power in the sky above or in the earth below—indeed, nothing in all creation will ever be able to separate us from the love of God that is revealed in Christ Jesus our Lord." (NLT)

Reflection: God's love is constant and unchanging. When you find your security in God's love, you no longer need to seek approval from others. Nothing can separate you from His love, and He accepts you just as you are. Rest in God's love and let it be the foundation of your confidence and security.

Journal Question: Is there anything you have been believing is able to separate you from God's love? Anything you have been allowing to define your worth other than God Himself?

Day 3: Replacing Negative Thoughts with Biblical Truth

Scripture: *2 Corinthians 10:5* - "We demolish arguments and every pretension that sets itself up against the knowledge of God, and we take captive every thought to make it obedient to Christ." (NIV)

Reflection: Your thoughts have a powerful impact on how you see yourself. If you're constantly dwelling on negative or insecure thoughts, it's time to replace them with God's truth. Take those thoughts captive and make them obedient to Christ. Instead of focusing on lies, meditate on what God says about you — that you are loved, valued, and chosen.

Journal Question: What negative thoughts do you need to take captive and replace with God's truth?

Day 4: Practical Ways to Build Self-Confidence in Christ

Scripture: *Philippians 4:13* - "I can do all things through Christ who strengthens me." (NKJV)

Reflection: Building self-confidence doesn't mean relying on your own abilities but trusting in God's strength. Find practical ways to grow in confidence, like spending time in prayer, reading God's Word, and surrounding yourself with encouraging people. As you grow in your relationship with God, your confidence will grow too, knowing that He equips you for every good work.

Journal Question: What is an area of your life that you could engage in more confidently if you were trusting God to give you what you need instead of looking at your own weaknesses?

Day 5: Surrounding Yourself with People Who Uplift You

Scripture: *Proverbs 27:17* - "As iron sharpens iron, so a friend sharpens a friend." (NLT)

Reflection: The people you spend time with have a big influence on how you see yourself. Surround yourself with friends who uplift you, encourage you, and speak God's truth into your life. When you're feeling insecure, let them remind you of your identity in Christ and support you in your journey of growth and confidence.

Journal Question: Who are the people in your life who uplift and encourage you, and how can you spend more time with them?

Weekly Summary

This week, we explored overcoming insecurity by recognizing your worth in God, finding security in His love, replacing negative thoughts with biblical truth, building self-confidence through Christ, and surrounding yourself with uplifting people. Your confidence comes not from the approval of others but from knowing who you are in God and letting His truth shape your view of yourself.

Real-Life Story

Lecrae: Finding Confidence in God's Truth Lecrae, now a famous Christian hip-hop and rap artist, faced significant struggles with identity and self-worth throughout his life, particularly during his formative years. Growing up in a challenging environment marked by instability, he dealt with issues like poverty and the absence of a father figure. These experiences contributed to feelings of confusion about his identity and low self-esteem.

As a teenager, Lecrae turned to various outlets, including music and hip-hop culture, seeking validation and a sense of belonging. However, he often found himself in destructive behaviors and a lifestyle that didn't align with his values, leading to deeper feelings of emptiness.

His transformative journey began when he encountered Christ in college. Through his faith, Lecrae discovered a new perspective on his identity. He learned that his worth wasn't tied to his past, his accomplishments, or the opinions of others, but rather rooted in being a child of God. This realization helped him embrace his true identity and value. Lecrae's faith journey fueled his passion for creating music that reflects his beliefs and experiences. He began to share his story through his lyrics, addressing themes of hope, redemption, and self-acceptance. As he grew in his faith, Lecrae gained confidence, recognizing that he was loved and chosen by God. His journey serves as a testament to the power of faith in transforming lives and reshaping identities (Lecrae, 2020).

Prayer

"God, thank You for creating me with purpose and value. Help me to overcome my insecurities and find my confidence in You. Remind me of Your truth when negative thoughts arise, and surround me with people who encourage me in my walk with You. Let my confidence be rooted in who You are and who You've made me to be. Amen."

WEEK 21

DEALING WITH FEAR AND ANXIETY

Practical Challenge

Find a verse that brings you peace and write it down somewhere you can see it daily. Whenever fear or anxiety arises, read that verse and let it remind you of God's presence, peace, and power over every situation.

Day 1: Understanding That Fear Is a Part of Life

Scripture: *John 16:33* - "'I have told you these things, so that in me you may have peace. In this world you will have trouble. But take heart! I have overcome the world.'" (NIV)

Reflection: Fear and anxiety are part of living in a fallen world, and it's okay to admit when you're struggling. Jesus tells us that we will face troubles and fears in this life, but He also reminds us that He has overcome the world. Let this promise bring you peace and hope, knowing that God is with you in your fears.

Journal Question: What fears or anxieties do you struggle with, and how have they affected your life?

Day 2: Trusting God in the Midst of Your Fears

Scripture: *Psalm 56:3-4* - "When I am afraid, I put my trust in you. In God, whose word I praise – in God I trust and am not afraid. What can mere mortals do to me?" (NIV)

Reflection: Trusting God doesn't mean never feeling fear; it means choosing to trust Him even when you do. When fear arises, put your trust in God's faithfulness, His love, and His ability to protect and guide you. Remember that God is bigger than any fear you face, and He is always present to give you peace.

Journal Question: How can you remind yourself of God's presence and strength when fear arises?

Day 3: Praying for Peace in Anxious Times

Scripture: *Philippians 4:6-7* - "Do not be anxious about anything, but in every situation, by prayer and petition, with thanksgiving, present your requests to God. 7 And the peace of God, which transcends all understanding, will guard your hearts and your minds in Christ Jesus." (NIV)

Reflection: When anxiety tries to take over, prayer is your greatest weapon. Bring all your worries, big or small, to God, and let His peace fill your heart. Prayer not only changes circumstances but also changes your perspective, helping you focus on God's power instead of your fears. Allow God's peace to guard your heart and mind in times of anxiety.

Journal Question: How can you intentionally hand your fears and anxieties over to God when they arise?

Day 4: Meditating on Scriptures That Calm Fear and Anxiety

Scripture: *Isaiah 41:10* - "So do not fear, for I am with you; do not be dismayed, for I am your God. I will strengthen you and help you; I will uphold you with my righteous right hand." (NIV)

Reflection: God's Word is filled with promises that bring comfort and calm in the midst of fear. Meditate on verses like Isaiah 41:10 that remind you of God's presence, strength, and love. Let these Scriptures be your anchor when fear and anxiety try to overwhelm you, and allow God's truth to bring peace to your soul.

Journal Question: What are some Scriptures that bring you comfort when you feel afraid or anxious?

Day 5: Developing Healthy Coping Mechanisms with God's Help

Scripture: *Romans 8:15* - "For you did not receive the spirit of bondage again to fear, but you received the Spirit of adoption by whom we cry out, 'Abba, Father.'" (NKJV)

Reflection: God gives you the power to face your fears and overcome anxiety. In addition to prayer and reading God's Word, developing healthy coping mechanisms, like deep breathing, journaling, exercising, and seeking good community, can help you deal with anxiety in a positive way. Ask God for wisdom and strength to develop habits that bring peace and healing, and rely on the Holy Spirit to help you live with courage and confidence.

Journal Question: What habits and coping mechanisms can you develop to help you handle anxiety in a healthy way? Ask the Holy Spirit for ideas.

Weekly Summary

This week, we focused on dealing with fear and anxiety by understanding that it's a part of life, trusting God in the midst of fear, praying for peace, meditating on calming Scriptures, and developing healthy coping mechanisms. God's presence and power are greater than any fear you face, and He wants to bring peace to your heart in every situation.

Real-Life Story

Max Lucado: Battling Fear with God's Truth Max Lucado, a Christian author and pastor, struggled with anxiety throughout his life. In his book *Anxious for Nothing*, Lucado has openly shared his struggles with anxiety, particularly during a challenging period in his life when he faced immense pressure as a pastor and author. He experienced feelings of being overwhelmed, leading to sleepless nights and a persistent sense of worry. This battle with anxiety caused him to question his abilities and left him feeling inadequate. In the midst of this struggle, Lucado turned to the Lord for strength and comfort. He found solace in Scripture, particularly verses that emphasize God's presence and reassurance. He began to meditate on passages that spoke to God's peace, such as Philippians 4:6-7, which encourages believers not to be anxious but to bring their concerns to God in prayer.

Through prayer and reflection, Lucado learned to replace his anxious thoughts with reminders of God's faithfulness. He developed practical strategies to cope with his anxiety, including journaling and deepening his prayer life. This process helped him to shift his focus from his fears to God's promises. Lucado writes, "The presence of anxiety is unavoidable, but the prison of anxiety is optional."

His story teaches that while fear and anxiety may be part of life, God's truth has the power to set you free and fill you with peace (Lucado, 2017).

Prayer

"God, thank You for being with me in my fears and anxieties. Help me to trust in Your power, love, and presence, and to find peace in You. When fear arises, remind me of Your promises and guide me in healthy ways to overcome anxiety. Let Your peace guard my heart and mind in every situation. Amen."

HANDLING STRESS

Practical Challenge

Create a daily routine that includes rest and time with God. Set aside time each day to pray, read the Bible, and rest in God's presence. Let this routine help you handle stress and experience God's peace.

Day 1: Identifying the Main Sources of Stress in Your Life

Scripture: *Matthew 11:28-29* - "Then Jesus said, 'Come to me, all of you who are weary and carry heavy burdens, and I will give you rest. Take my yoke upon you. Let me teach you, because I am humble and gentle at heart, and you will find rest for your souls.'" (NLT)

Reflection: Stress comes in many forms — school pressure, sports, relationships, and personal expectations. But Jesus invites you to bring all your burdens to Him and find rest. Identifying the sources of stress in your life is the first step to finding peace. When you know what is weighing you down, you can bring those burdens to Jesus and allow Him to give you rest and renewal.

Journal Question: What are the main sources of stress in your life, and how can you bring them to God for peace?

Day 2: The Importance of Rest and Time with God

Scripture: *Isaiah 30:15* - "This is what the Sovereign Lord, the Holy One of Israel, says: 'Only in returning to me and resting in me will you be saved. In quietness and confidence is your strength...'" (NLT)

Reflection: In the midst of a busy and stressful life, God calls you to be still. Taking time to rest, pray, and spend time with God is essential for finding peace. Rest is not just about taking a break from activities — it's about finding rest in God's presence. Make time each day to be still, connect with God, and let Him fill you with His peace.

Journal Question: How can you structure your days and your weeks in a way that creates intentional time for you to rest with the Lord?

Day 3: How to Manage Your Time Effectively to Reduce Stress

Scripture: *Ephesians 5:15-16* - "So be careful how you live. Don't live like fools, but like those who are wise. Make the most of every opportunity in these evil days." (NLT)

Reflection: Stress can come from feeling overwhelmed by everything you need to do, but it can be even worse if there is a disconnect between what is taking up most of your time and what is actually the most valuable to you. Managing your time effectively helps you reduce stress and make the most of your days. Set priorities based on what actually matters to you the most, make a schedule, and make sure to plan time for rest and God-time. When you use your time wisely, you can accomplish more and experience greater peace.

Journal Question: What are some practical ways you can manage your time more effectively to reduce stress? Are there any things that are taking up a lot of your time that are not actually worth spending so much time on?

Day 4: Practical Tips for Handling School, Sports, and Other Pressures

Scripture: *Isaiah 40:31* - "But those who trust in the Lord will find new strength. They will soar high on wings like eagles. They will run and not grow weary. They will walk and not faint." (NLT)

Reflection: Balancing school, sports, family, and friends can be stressful, but God gives you the strength to handle the things He brings your way. Ask Him if there is any activity or relationship you have been committing time to that is not something He wants you to be prioritizing right now. If so, be willing to let that thing go. Then, set realistic goals, ask for help when you need it, and don't be afraid to take breaks when you're feeling overwhelmed. Remember that God is your strength, and if you are leaning into Him, He will give you what you need each day.

Journal Question: Are there any areas of your life where you have been plowing ahead in your own strength instead of inviting God to give you what you need? Are there any commitments that God is asking you to surrender and not spend time on anymore right now?

Day 5: Trusting God with Your Worries

Scripture: *1 Peter 5:7* - "Give all your worries and cares to God, for he cares about you." (NLT)

Reflection: God cares deeply about what you're going through, and He wants you to bring all your worries and stress to Him. When you cast your anxiety on God, you're not just letting go of your burdens — you're putting them into the hands of the One who loves you and is able to help you. Trust God with your worries and find comfort in knowing that He is always with you.

Journal Question: What worries do you need to cast on God, and how can you trust Him more with your burdens?

Weekly Summary

This week, we focused on handling stress by identifying its sources, finding rest in God, managing your time wisely, handling pressures effectively, and trusting God with your worries. Stress is a normal part of life, but God offers peace, strength, and guidance through every situation. Lean on Him, and let Him bring you rest.

Real-Life Story

Tim Tebow: Handling Stress Through Faith Tim Tebow, former NFL quarterback and current sports commentator, faced immense pressure on and off the field throughout his career. However, Tebow consistently emphasized that his identity is rooted in his faith in God rather than in his performance on the field. This mindset helped him avoid feeling overwhelmed by the constant scrutiny of his career, whether as a Heisman Trophy-winning college quarterback, an NFL player, or a professional baseball player. In the face of criticism, stress, and high expectations, Tebow leaned on his faith. He once said, "No matter how much stress or pressure you're under, know that God is always with you" (Tebow, 2016). This perspective helped shield him from the emotional highs and lows associated with public opinion. Tim's example shows that, by placing your trust in God, you can handle life's pressures with confidence, peace, and perseverance.

Prayer

"God, thank You for being with me in the midst of my stress. Help me to bring my burdens to You, find rest in Your presence, and trust in Your strength to handle the pressures I face. Teach me to manage my time and my priorities wisely and to lean on You for peace in every situation. Amen."

DEVELOPING SELF-DISCIPLINE

Practical Challenge

Set one spiritual goal for yourself this week and create a plan to stick to it. Whether it's a daily prayer time, Bible reading plan, serving others, or continuing the challenge from last week, commit to your goal and ask God for the discipline to see it through.

Day 1: Why Self-Discipline Is Important for Spiritual Growth

Scripture: *1 Corinthians 9:24-25* - "Don't you realize that in a race everyone runs, but only one person gets the prize? So run to win! All athletes are disciplined in their training. They do it to win a prize that will fade away, but we do it for an eternal prize." (NLT)

Reflection: Just like an athlete trains with discipline to win a race, spiritual growth requires self-discipline. Practicing habits like prayer, Bible reading, worship, and serving others helps you grow closer to God and develop spiritual maturity. Self-discipline is not about being perfect but about making consistent choices that lead you toward God and His purpose for your life.

Journal Question: What are some areas in your life where you need to develop more self-discipline?

Day 2: Setting Goals and Sticking to Them

Scripture: *Proverbs 21:5* - "Good planning and hard work lead to prosperity, but hasty shortcuts lead to poverty." (NLT)

Reflection: Setting goals is a powerful way to develop self-discipline. Whether it's reading your Bible more, praying regularly, or setting boundaries in your relationships, goals help you stay focused and motivated. Be diligent in pursuing the goals God places on your heart, and ask Him for the strength to stick to them even when it's challenging.

Journal Question: Ask the Lord if there are any goals He would like you to set for yourself. Did anything come to mind?

Day 3: Overcoming Laziness and Procrastination

Scripture: *Proverbs 13:4* - "Lazy people want much but get little, but those who work hard will prosper." (NLT)

Reflection: Laziness and procrastination can keep you from growing and reaching your full potential. God calls you to be diligent and use your time wisely, honoring Him in all you do. When you feel like putting things off, ask God for motivation and focus to complete the tasks He has given you. Remember, self-discipline leads to satisfaction and growth.

Journal Question: What are some strategies you can use to overcome procrastination and be diligent in the tasks God has given you?

Day 4: Learning to Say "No" to Distractions

Scripture: *2 Timothy 2:4-7* - "Soldiers don't get tied up in the affairs of civilian life, for then they cannot please the officer who enlisted them. And athletes cannot win the prize unless they follow the rules. And hardworking farmers should be the first to enjoy the fruit of their labor. Think about what I am saying. The Lord will help you understand all these things." (NLT)

Reflection: Distractions are everywhere — whether it's social media, entertainment, or things that take your focus away from God's purpose. Learning to say "no" to distractions allows you to stay on the path God has set for you. Run your race with perseverance by setting aside anything that hinders you from growing in your relationship with God and from accomplishing the unique purpose He has for your life.

Journal Question: What distractions often keep you from spending time with God or reaching your goals?

Day 5: How to Grow in Self-Discipline with God's Help

Scripture: *Philippians 2:13* - "For God is working in you, giving you the desire and the power to do what pleases him." (NLT)

Reflection: Self-discipline is not something you have to do alone. God is at work in you, helping you to desire to follow His will. Ask God for help to develop self-discipline, and rely on His strength and guidance. As you grow in self-discipline, you'll find that your actions align more with God's purpose, and your relationship with Him deepens.

Journal Question: Are there any areas in your life where you should ask God to influence your will or desires so that they will better line up with His will and desires?

Weekly Summary

This week, we focused on developing self-discipline as a key part of spiritual growth. By setting goals, overcoming laziness, saying no to distractions, and relying on God's help, you can grow in self-discipline and become more like Christ. Self-discipline is not just about avoiding bad habits but about pursuing the things that lead you closer to God and His purpose for your life.

Real-Life Story

Hudson Taylor: A Life of Spiritual Discipline Hudson Taylor, a missionary to China and the founder of the China Inland Mission, was known not only for his pioneering work in missions but also for his deep spiritual disciplines. Taylor practiced consistent daily habits of prayer, Bible reading, and fasting, which gave him strength to face the challenges of his ministry. He once said, "Do not have your concert first and tune your instruments afterward.

Begin the day with God" (Taylor, 1997). His life demonstrated that spiritual disciplines are not burdens but pathways to deeper intimacy with God and greater strength for His work. Taylor's story encourages us to make spiritual disciplines a priority and to seek God first in everything we do.

Prayer

"God, thank You for working in me to fulfill Your purpose. Help me to develop self-discipline, to set goals that honor You, and to overcome distractions and laziness. Teach me to rely on Your strength as I pursue spiritual growth and draw closer to You. Amen."

NAVIGATING SOCIAL MEDIA AND SELF-WORTH

Practical Challenge

Choose one way to use your social media to spread encouragement and positivity this week. It could be sharing an uplifting Bible verse, sending a kind message to a friend, or posting something that reflects God's love and truth.

Day 1: How Social Media Can Influence Your Self-Image

Scripture: *2 Corinthians 10:12,17-18* - "...But they are only comparing themselves with each other, using themselves as the standard of measurement. How ignorant! As the Scriptures say, 'If you want to boast, boast only about the Lord.' When people commend themselves, it doesn't count for much. The important thing is for the Lord to commend them." (NLT)

Reflection: Social media is a powerful tool, but it can also negatively affect your self-image. It's easy to compare yourself to others and seek approval through likes, comments, or followers. But God wants your identity to be rooted in Him, not in the opinions of others. Remember that God's approval is what matters most, and your worth is found in Him.

Journal Question: How has social media influenced the way you see yourself, and how can you find your worth in God instead?

Day 2: Finding Your Worth in God, Not in Likes or Followers

Scripture: *Zephaniah 3:17* - "For the Lord your God is living among you. He is a mighty savior. He will take delight in you with gladness. With his love, he will calm all your fears. He will rejoice over you with joyful songs." (NLT)

Reflection: Your value is not determined by how many likes, followers, or comments you receive on social media. Your worth is found in God, who loves you unconditionally and delights in you. When you're tempted to measure your worth by social media, remember that God literally sings about you, and His love for you doesn't change based on how popular you are.

Journal Question: Think of a time when you allowed someone's reaction to you on social media to affect your feeling of self-worth. Now ask God to show you what He was thinking about you in that same moment. What did He show you?

Day 3: Setting Healthy Boundaries with Social Media Use

Scripture: *1 Corinthians 6:12* - "'I have the right to do anything,' you say—but not everything is beneficial. 'I have the right to do anything'—but I will not be mastered by anything." (NIV)

Reflection: While social media can be a fun way to connect with others, it's important to set boundaries to prevent it from consuming your time or affecting your mental health. Decide on limits for how much time you spend online and be mindful of what you're viewing. Don't let social media master you or influence your self-worth or your opinions of the world and people around you — instead, let God's truth be your guide.

Journal Question: What are some healthy boundaries you can set to limit your time and focus on social media?

Day 4: Avoiding Comparison with Others Online

Scripture: *Isaiah 25:1* - "Lord, you are my God; I will exalt you and praise your name, for in perfect faithfulness you have done wonderful things, things planned long ago." (NIV)

Reflection: It's easy to fall into the trap of comparing your life to others on social media. Remember that what you see online is often a highlight reel, not reality. God created you uniquely, with your own path and purpose. Instead of comparing yourself to others, focus on who God has called you to be and celebrate the unique gifts and blessings He's given you. Look back on His faithfulness throughout your life and remember the ways He has been intentionally growing you, encouraging you, and loving you.

Journal Question: How can you avoid comparing yourself to others online and celebrate who God created you to be? What are three things God has done in your life that you are grateful for today?

Day 5: Using Social Media to Positively Impact Others

Scripture: *Psalm 71:15-16* - "I will tell everyone about your righteousness. All day long I will proclaim your saving power, though I am not skilled with words. I will praise your mighty deeds, O Sovereign Lord. I will tell everyone that you alone are just." (NLT)

Reflection: Social media can be a platform for sharing God's love, truth, and encouragement and for proclaiming the power of His redemptive work in your life. Use your online presence to be a light to others — share positive messages, encourage your friends, and reflect God's love in all you post. When you let your light shine, others can see the goodness of God through your actions and words, and your testimony of God's faithfulness can inspire others to trust Him.

Journal Question: What are some ways you can use your social media presence to encourage and positively impact others? How can you let your online presence be a reflection of God's love and truth?

Weekly Summary

This week, we focused on navigating social media and self-worth. Social media can have a big influence on your self-image if you let it, but God calls you to find your worth in Him. By setting healthy boundaries, avoiding comparison, and using social media as a tool for positive impact, you can navigate the online world in a way that honors God, guards your own heart, and builds up others.

Real-Life Story

Sadie Robertson Huff: Using Social Media for God's Glory Sadie Robertson Huff, a Christian author, speaker, and social media influencer, who largely gained influence through her appearance on the reality TV show *Duck Dynasty*, is known for using her online platform to spread faith, positivity, and encouragement. She's faced pressure from social media but learned to find her worth in God instead of likes or followers. Sadie says, "Don't let social media be the place you find your worth; let it be the place you show others where they can find theirs" (Huff, 2020). Her life shows that when you use social media with purpose, it can be a powerful tool to glorify God and uplift others.

Prayer

"God, thank You for loving me and giving me worth that isn't based on social media or the opinions of others. Help me to set healthy boundaries, avoid comparison, and use my online presence to reflect Your love and truth. Let me find my worth in You and be a light to others, both online and offline. Amen."

EMBRACING GOD'S PURPOSE FOR YOUR LIFE

Practical Challenge

Pray this week for God to reveal His purpose for your life. Ask Him to show you how to use your gifts to serve others and to guide you step by step in His perfect plan. Look for small opportunities to act on God's purpose each day.

Day 1: Discovering Your God-Given Talents and Abilities

Scripture: *1 Peter 4:10* - "God has given each of you a gift from his great variety of spiritual gifts. Use them well to serve one another." (NLT)

Reflection: God has given you unique talents, abilities, and passions that He wants to use for His kingdom. Discovering what you're good at and what you enjoy doing is part of understanding God's purpose for your life. Pray for God to show you the gifts He's given you and seek ways to use them to serve others and bring glory to Him.

Journal Question: What are some talents and abilities God has given you, and how can you use them for His glory?

Day 2: How to Seek God's Will for Your Life

Scripture: *Matthew 6:33* - "But seek first his kingdom and his righteousness, and all these things will be given to you as well." (NIV)

Reflection: Seeking God's will begins with making Him your top priority. When you choose to seek God's kingdom and righteousness first, everything else in your life falls into place. This doesn't mean you'll always have every answer immediately, but it does mean that as you align your desires with God's heart, He will guide your path. Trust that when you put God first, He will reveal His will and provide for every need one step at a time.

Journal Question: How can you seek God's will for your life through prayer, Bible study, and wise counsel?

Day 3: Being Patient in Finding Your Purpose

Scripture: *Psalm 37:7* - "Be still in the presence of the Lord, and wait patiently for him to act. Don't worry about evil people who prosper or fret about their wicked schemes." (NLT)

Reflection: Finding God's purpose for your life often requires patience. It's easy to get frustrated or compare yourself to others who seem to know what they're doing, but God's timing is perfect. Be patient and trust that God is working in your life, even when you can't see the full picture. Remember that waiting on God is part of the journey toward discovering His purpose.

Journal Question: What areas of your life require patience as you wait on God's purpose to unfold?

Day 4: Trusting God Even When His Plan is Unclear

Scripture: *Psalm 138:8* - "The Lord will work out his plans for my life— for your faithful love, O Lord, endures forever. Don't abandon me, for you made me." (NLT)

Reflection: Sometimes, God's plan for your life may seem unclear or different from what you expected. But God's plans are always good, and He sees the bigger picture that you may not understand. Trust in God's character, knowing that He has a plan and purpose for your life that is perfect and born out of His love for you. Let your faith be rooted in God's goodness, even when you don't have all the answers.

Journal Question: What areas of your life right now do you have the opportunity to trust God's plan even when it seems unclear or different from your own?

Day 5: Taking Small Steps Toward Fulfilling Your Purpose

Scripture: *Colossians 3:23* - "Whatever you do, work at it with all your heart, as working for the Lord, not for human masters," (NIV)

Reflection: Fulfilling God's purpose doesn't happen all at once — it's a journey of taking small, faithful steps. Whether you're serving in your church, working hard at school, or helping a friend, do everything with a heart to honor God. Each step you take in obedience and faithfulness brings you closer to fulfilling God's purpose for your life.

Journal Question: What small steps can you take today to move closer to fulfilling God's purpose for your life?

Weekly Summary

This week, we explored how to embrace God's purpose for your life by discovering your gifts, seeking God's will, being patient, trusting God's plan, and taking small steps in obedience. God has a unique purpose for you, and as you trust Him, take steps of faith, and rely on His guidance, you'll find the path He's laid out for you.

Real-Life Story

Lottie Moon: Embracing God's Purpose in Missions Lottie Moon was a missionary to China who dedicated her life to sharing the gospel with the Chinese people. Lottie Moon's call to serve in China came during a transformative period in her life. As a young woman, she was well-educated and initially skeptical of Christianity, even mocking religious gatherings. However, during a revival meeting at her college, she experienced a profound change of heart and committed her life to Christ. This decision sparked a desire to serve God in a deeper way.

In 1873, while working as a teacher, Lottie began to feel a strong burden for missions, especially for those who had never heard the gospel. She became captivated by stories of China's vast, unreached population and realized that few missionaries were ministering to Chinese women, who had little chance to hear the gospel. Despite her family's doubts and society's limited acceptance of women missionaries, she felt an undeniable call to go.

Lottie finally answered God's call and traveled to China, where she devoted over 40 years of her life to sharing the gospel, teaching, and advocating for missions. Her commitment and sacrifices, including giving away her own food during times of famine, left a legacy that continues to inspire missionary work today. Despite facing loneliness, hardship, and illness, she embraced God's purpose with faith and determination. Lottie once said, "I have a firm conviction that I am immortal till my work is done" (Cannon, 1997). Her passion to serve others and fulfill God's calling on her life left a lasting impact on missions around the world. Lottie's story reminds us that when we embrace God's purpose, we can make a difference that lasts beyond our lifetime.

Prayer

"God, thank You for giving me unique gifts and a purpose. Help me to discover the talents You've given me, to seek Your will, and to trust in Your plan for my life. Teach me to be patient in the journey and to take small steps of obedience toward fulfilling Your purpose. Use my life for Your glory and to serve others. Amen."

BALANCING SCHOOL, FRIENDS, AND FAITH

Practical Challenge

Choose one area of your life where you need to manage your time better and set a goal for improvement this week. Ask God for wisdom in prioritizing your time, and commit to making changes that help you grow closer to Him and balance your life well.

Day 1: Setting Priorities to Keep God First

Scripture: *Matthew 22:37-38* - "Jesus replied, '"You must love the Lord your God with all your heart, all your soul, and all your mind." This is the first and greatest commandment.'" (NLT)

Reflection: In the midst of all your responsibilities — school, sports, friendships — it's easy to let your relationship with God take a back seat. But Jesus reminds us that the greatest priority in life is to love God first. When you set God as your number one priority, everything else falls into place. Start each day by seeking Him, and let your love for God guide your decisions and actions.

Journal Question: What are your top priorities based on how you spend your time and energy, and how can you make sure God is first in your life?

Day 2: How to Manage Your Time Effectively

Scripture: *Colossians 4:5* - "Walk in wisdom toward those *who are* outside, redeeming the time." (NKJV)

Reflection: Managing your time wisely allows you to balance school, friends, and faith without feeling overwhelmed. Make the most of every opportunity by setting aside time for studying, spending time with friends, and growing in your relationship with God. Create a schedule that honors God and helps you make the most of each day.

Journal Question: How can you create a schedule that helps you balance school, friends, and faith?

Day 3: Making Sure Faith is a Priority in a Busy Schedule

Scripture: *Psalm 119:105* - "Your word *is* a lamp to my feet and a light to my path." (NKJV)

Reflection: With all the busyness of life, it's important to make sure your faith remains a priority. Spending time in God's Word and prayer will help guide your steps and keep your focus on Him. Even a few minutes a day can make a big difference in staying connected to God. Let His Word light your path as you navigate your busy schedule.

Journal Question: What are some practical ways you can make spending time with the Lord a priority, even on busy days?

Day 4: Finding Balance Between School, Friends, and Activities

Scripture: *Ecclesiastes 3:1* - "For everything there is a season, a time for every activity under heaven." (NLT)

Reflection: Life has different seasons, and finding balance means recognizing what's important in each one. There will be times to focus on schoolwork, to hang out with friends, and to deepen your faith. Balance is not about doing everything perfectly but about understanding that God has given you a season for every activity. Trust Him to help you find the right balance for your life in this specific season.

Journal Question: How can you recognize the season you're in and find balance in your activities?

Day 5: Relying on God's Strength When Life Feels Overwhelming

Scripture: *Isaiah 40:29* - "He gives strength to the weary and increases the power of the weak." (NIV)

Reflection: When life feels overwhelming, and you're struggling to balance everything, remember that God is your source of strength. He is ready to give you the power and endurance you need for each day. Lean on Him when you're tired or stressed, and trust that He will carry you through every season.

Journal Question: What is an area of your life that has felt overwhelming recently? Invite God into that situation and ask for His wisdom and strength. What do you hear Him saying?

Weekly Summary

This week, we explored how to balance school, friends, and faith by setting priorities, managing your time, making faith a priority, finding balance between activities, and relying on God's strength. Life can be busy, but with God's help, you can find balance and honor Him in every area.

Real-Life Story

Bethany Hamilton: Finding Balance Through Faith One of the most powerful moments of Bethany Hamilton finding peace amidst chaos happened right after her shark attack in 2003. Bethany, a 13-year-old competitive surfer, was attacked by a 14-foot tiger shark while surfing off the coast of Hawaii, losing her left arm in an instant. The traumatic event not only threatened her life but also put her surfing dreams in jeopardy.

In the hospital, as she faced the gravity of her injury, Bethany was overwhelmed with fear and uncertainty. Yet, she turned to God, praying for strength and comfort. Amidst the chaos, she felt an unexplainable sense of peace and purpose. Bethany leaned on the Bible verse *"I can do all things through Christ who strengthens me"* (Philippians 4:13), which became her anchor during recovery.

With this peace guiding her, she returned to surfing just a month after the attack, learning to balance and ride the waves with one arm. Her resilience and unwavering faith inspired people around the world, showing that even in the face of incredible loss and chaos, peace and strength can be found through Jesus. This tragedy didn't stop her from pursuing her dreams of surfing competitively, and today, despite her busy schedule of surfing, competitions, and public speaking, she remains committed to her faith. Bethany often shares that finding balance starts with making God the center of everything: "When you put God first, everything else falls into place" (Hamilton, 2004). Her story encourages us to seek God's help in balancing life's responsibilities and to find peace by making time with the Lord a priority.

Prayer

"God, thank You for giving me the opportunity to learn, grow, and build relationships. Help me to balance my time wisely and to make You my number one priority. When life feels busy or overwhelming, remind me to rely on Your strength and to keep my focus on You. Amen."

Make a Difference with Your Review

Unlock the Power of Generosity

"Give, and you will receive. Your gift will return to you in full—pressed down, shaken together to make room for more, running over, and poured into your lap. The amount you give will determine the amount you get back." — Luke 6:38 (NLT)

People who give without expecting anything in return live more joyful lives. So, let's make a difference together!

Would you help someone just like you — a teen boy looking for guidance, unsure where to begin - find *The Ultimate Devotional for Teen Boys*? My mission is to make this devotional accessible to every teen boy seeking to grow in his faith, manage stress, and find his identity in God. But to reach more readers, I need your help.

Most people choose books based on reviews. So, I'm asking you to help another teen by leaving your thoughts. It takes just a minute, but your review could change someone's spiritual journey. Your words could help one more young person find hope; help one more boy navigate relationships with God, himself, and others; help one more teen realize his identity in Christ; and help one more life be transformed through intentional time in God's word.

To make a difference, simply scan the QR code and leave a review. Thank you for being a part of this journey and for helping others grow in faith!

WEEK 27

STAYING PURE IN HEART AND MIND

Practical Challenge

Choose one area of your life where you need to practice purity, whether it's in your thoughts, media choices, or actions. Make a commitment this week to guard your heart, seek God's help in overcoming temptation, and live in a way that honors Him.

Day 1: Why Purity Matters to God

Scripture: *Matthew 5:8* - "Blessed *are* the pure in heart, for they shall see God." (NKJV)

Reflection: Purity isn't just about what you do — it's about the state of your heart. God desires for you to live in purity because it brings you closer to Him and helps you reflect His character to the world. A pure heart seeks to honor God in all things, leading to a deeper relationship with Him. Choose to live in purity and experience the blessing of seeing God more clearly.

Journal Question: Why does purity matter to God and how does it help you grow closer to Him?

Day 2: Guarding Your Heart Against Negative Influences

Scripture: *Proverbs 4:23* - "Above all else, guard your heart, for everything you do flows from it." (NIV)

Reflection: Your heart is the source of your thoughts, actions, and decisions, so it's important to guard it against negative influences. Be mindful of what you watch, listen to, and expose yourself to. Surround yourself with things that uplift you and encourage your faith, and protect your heart from anything that draws you away from God's truth.

Journal Question: What are some negative influences in your life that you need to guard your heart against? How can you remove or reduce your exposure to those influences?

Day 3: How to Maintain Purity in What You Watch, Read, and Listen To

Scripture: *Philippians 4:8* - "And now, dear brothers and sisters, one final thing. Fix your thoughts on what is true, and honorable, and right, and pure, and lovely, and admirable. Think about things that are excellent and worthy of praise." (NLT)

Reflection: The media you consume has a big impact on your thoughts and heart. Choose to watch, read, and listen to things that are pure and uplifting. Let God's Word be your standard for what you allow into your mind and heart. When you fill your mind with things that are true, noble, and pure, you protect your heart and stay close to God.

Journal Question: How can you be intentional about choosing pure things to watch, read, and listen to? Is there anyone you can invite to keep you accountable in this area?

Day 4: Overcoming Temptations Through Prayer and Scripture

Scripture: *1 Corinthians 10:13* - "The temptations in your life are no different from what others experience. And God is faithful. He will not allow the temptation to be more than you can stand. When you are tempted, he will show you a way out so that you can endure." (NLT)

Reflection: Temptation is a normal part of life, but God promises to help you overcome it. Through prayer and meditating on Scripture, you can find strength to resist temptation and choose purity. God is faithful and provides a way out of every situation where you are tempted. Rely on His strength and truth when you face temptation. Look for the way out that He has provided.

Journal Question: Think about a temptation you faced recently. What was the "way of escape" that God provided in that situation? Did you take it?

Day 5: Developing Pure Thoughts and Actions

Scripture: *Psalm 51:10* - "Create in me a pure heart, O God, and renew a steadfast spirit within me." (NIV)

Reflection: Developing a pure heart begins with asking God to renew your thoughts and actions. Pray for God to cleanse your heart and help you desire what is good, pure, and holy. As you draw closer to God, He will transform your thoughts, renew your mind, and help you live a life of purity that honors Him.

Journal Question: What is an area in your life where you do not currently see yourself desiring what is pure? Invite God to begin changing your desires in that area to align with His heart.

Weekly Summary

This week, we focused on staying pure in heart and mind by understanding why purity matters to God, guarding your heart against negative influences, choosing pure media, overcoming temptations through prayer, and developing pure thoughts and actions. Purity is not just about what you avoid — it's about living in a way that honors God in all areas of your life.

Real-Life Story

Elisabeth Elliot: Pursuing Purity of Heart and Mind Elisabeth Elliot, a missionary, author, and speaker, was known for her commitment to living a life of purity and holiness. Elisabeth chose and championed purity while waiting to marry Jim Elliot by embracing a deep commitment to God's timing and principles. She and Jim met in college and had a strong connection and desire to marry, but Jim felt called to remain single at the time and move to the mission field in Ecuador, not knowing whether God would give him the freedom to marry later on. During this period, Elisabeth remained faithful to her Christian beliefs, focusing on spiritual growth, prayer, and trusting that God would lead them in the right direction. She upheld the values of purity and patience, believing that God's will was more important than their immediate desires. She once said, "Holiness has never been the driving force of the majority. It is, however, mandatory for anyone who wants to enter the kingdom" (Elliott, 1989, *Gate of Splendor*). Elisabeth and Jim did finally marry, and when they did, their relationship was built on a foundation of shared faith, trust in God's timing, and mutual commitment to purity. Elisabeth's life reminds us that living a pure life is about pursuing God above all else (Elliot, 2003).

Prayer

"God, thank You for calling me to live a life of purity. Help me to guard my heart, choose pure influences, and overcome temptations with Your strength. Create in me a pure heart, and help me to live in a way that honors and glorifies You. Amen."

Week 28

Body Image and Self-Esteem

Practical Challenge

Write down three qualities that God values in you that are not related to your appearance. Focus on developing these qualities throughout the week and remind yourself that your worth comes from God, not from how you look.

Day 1: Understanding That You Are Made in God's Image

Scripture: *Genesis 1:27* - "So God created human beings in his own image. In the image of God he created them; male and female he created them." (NLT)

Reflection: Your body is a gift from God, made in His image. This means you are a reflection of God's creativity and love. The world may try to tell you that your worth is based on appearance, but your true value comes from being made in God's image. Embrace the fact that you are uniquely and wonderfully created by Him.

Journal Question: How does knowing you are made in God's image change the way you see yourself?

Day 2: Rejecting Society's False Standards of Value in Physical Appearance

Scripture: *1 Samuel 16:7* - "But the Lord said to Samuel, 'Don't judge by his appearance or height, for I have rejected him. The Lord doesn't see things the way you see them. People judge by outward appearance, but the Lord looks at the heart.'" (NLT)

Reflection: The world often promotes a standard of value in physical appearance that is unrealistic and unattainable. But God sees past the outward appearance and looks at your heart. He values your character, kindness, faith, and love more than anything else. When you feel pressure to look a certain way, remember that God cares about who you are on the inside.

Journal Question: What false standards of physical appearance do you feel pressure to live up to, and how can you reject them?

Day 3: Learning to Love and Care for Your Body

Scripture: *1 Corinthians 6:19-20* - "Don't you realize that your body is the temple of the Holy Spirit, who lives in you and was given to you by God? You do not belong to yourself, for God bought you with a high price. So you must honor God with your body." (NLT)

Reflection: Your body is not only a creation of God but a temple of the Holy Spirit. This means you should take care of it, not out of vanity, but as an act of honoring God. Eating well, exercising, resting, and being mindful of what you allow into your body are all ways to love and care for the body God has given you.

Journal Question: How can you care for your body in a way that honors God and reflects His love for you?

Day 4: Focusing on Your Character, Not Just Appearance

Scripture: *1 Samuel 13:14* - "But now your kingdom [Saul] will not endure; the Lord has sought out a man after his own heart and appointed him ruler of his people, because you have not kept the Lord's command.'" (NIV, *brackets added*)

Reflection: God chose David, a young shepherd boy, to replace Saul as King of Israel, not because of his outward appearance or physical strength but because of his heart. David was a man after God's own heart, and God valued David's character, love for Him, and desire to follow His ways. In a world that often focuses on appearance, remember that God values who you are on the inside. Strive to be a person after God's own heart, developing character that honors Him.

Journal Question: What qualities and character traits are more important to God than physical appearance? How can you grow and develop those qualities?

Day 5: Finding Self-Esteem in God's Approval, Not Others

Scripture: *Galatians 1:10* - "Obviously, I'm not trying to win the approval of people, but of God. If pleasing people were my goal, I would not be Christ's servant." (NLT)

Reflection: It's easy to let others' opinions shape how you see yourself, but God's approval is what truly matters. You are loved, valued, and accepted by God just as you are. Let your self-esteem come from knowing who you are in Christ and not from trying to fit into the world's standards.

Journal Question: Where is an area of your life that you can see yourself trying to please people more than please God? Bring that to the Lord in repentance and ask for God's help to seek His approval over people's approval.

Weekly Summary

This week, we explored body image and self-esteem from a biblical perspective. You are made in God's image, and your value is not based on appearance but on who God says you are. By focusing on your character, caring for your body, and finding self-esteem in God's approval, you can develop a healthy view of yourself that honors God.

Real-Life Story

Samantha Ponder: Finding True Beauty and Worth in Christ Samantha Ponder's journey toward valuing her character and inner beauty more than external appearances began during her time in college. Like many young women, she faced the pressures of societal standards regarding beauty and success, particularly in the competitive world of sports media. She often felt the weight of expectations to look a certain way and to be perfect on camera.

One pivotal moment came during her internship with ESPN, where she was eager to impress and make a name for herself. She found herself in a high-pressure environment, surrounded by established professionals and facing criticism about her appearance. In the midst of trying to fit into this world, Samantha began to lose sight of who she truly was and what she valued most. Feeling disheartened, she turned to her faith for guidance. In prayer and reflection, Samantha began to understand that her worth was not defined by how others perceived her or by her physical appearance. She realized that her character, kindness, and authenticity were far more valuable than any external validation. This revelation sparked a transformation in her approach to her career and life.

Samantha began to focus on being genuine and uplifting rather than conforming to the pressures of the industry. She shared her faith openly, emphasizing the importance of inner strength and resilience. Her confidence grew as she recognized that her true beauty came from being a person of integrity, compassion, and faith. Through her platform, Samantha now encourages others to embrace their worth based on character rather than external appearances. She uses her voice to advocate for authenticity and self-acceptance, inspiring countless individuals to prioritize their inner beauty and to find strength in their identity as valued children of God (Sharp, 2024).

Prayer

"God, thank You for making me in Your image. Help me to reject society's standards of beauty and to find my worth in You. Teach me to care for my body as a temple of Your Spirit, and let my self-esteem be rooted in who You say I am. Help me to focus on my character and live in a way that honors You. Amen."

DEALING WITH FAILURE

Practical Challenge

Choose one past failure or mistake and pray for God's wisdom and grace to move forward from it. Ask Him to show you what you can learn from it and how you can use it as an opportunity for growth.

Day 1: Understanding That Failure Is Part of Life

Scripture: *Proverbs 24:16* - "The godly may trip seven times, but they will get up again. But one disaster is enough to overthrow the wicked." (NLT)

Reflection: Failure is inevitable, and everyone experiences it at some point in life. But God doesn't see failure as the end — He sees it as an opportunity to grow, learn, and rise again. When you fail, don't be discouraged or give up. Instead, see it as a chance to trust God, learn from your mistakes, and keep moving forward.

Journal Question: How have you experienced failure in your life, and what did you learn from it?

Day 2: How to Learn from Your Mistakes

Scripture: *James 1:5* - "If any of you lacks wisdom, you should ask God, who gives generously to all without finding fault, and it will be given to you." (NIV)

Reflection: Mistakes can be some of life's greatest teachers if you choose to learn from them. When you make a mistake, ask God for wisdom to understand what went wrong and how to grow from it. God doesn't hold your failures against you; instead, He offers grace, guidance, and a chance to learn and become wiser.

Journal Question: Are there any mistakes or failures that you do not feel you have learned anything from yet? Bring those experiences to the Lord one at a time and ask for His wisdom to see the growth that can come from those experiences so you can move forward as a wiser person.

Day 3: God's Grace When We Fail

Scripture: *2 Corinthians 12:9* - "But he said to me, 'My grace is sufficient for you, for my power is made perfect in weakness.' Therefore I will boast all the more gladly about my weaknesses, so that Christ's power may rest on me." (NIV)

Reflection: God's grace is there to catch you when you fail. He doesn't expect perfection — He desires your heart and willingness to follow Him. When you're weak or struggling, God's grace is strong enough to cover your failures and carry you through. Let His grace remind you that your worth isn't based on your success but on His love for you.

Journal Question: What is a time you have seen God's grace encourage you when you failed or fallen short?

Day 4: Moving Forward After Failure

Scripture: *Philippians 3:13-14* - "Brothers and sisters, I do not consider myself yet to have taken hold of it. But one thing I do: Forgetting what is behind and straining toward what is ahead, I press on toward the goal to win the prize for which God has called me heavenward in Christ Jesus." (NIV)

Reflection: When you experience failure, don't stay stuck in the past. God calls you to move forward, learn from your mistakes, and keep striving toward His purpose for your life. Let go of what's behind you, and press on toward what God has ahead. With each step forward, you grow stronger in your faith and closer to the person God created you to be.

Journal Question: What are some ways you can move forward after failure, instead of staying stuck in the past? Is there a specific area of your life where you need to ask God to help you do this?

Day 5: Turning Failure into an Opportunity for Growth

Scripture: *Romans 5:3-4* - "We can rejoice, too, when we run into problems and trials, for we know that they help us develop endurance. And endurance develops strength of character, and character strengthens our confident hope of salvation." (NLT)

Reflection: Failure can be a catalyst for growth if you choose to see it that way. The challenges, setbacks, and struggles you face can develop perseverance, character, and hope within you. Ask God to use your failures as opportunities to shape your character and help you grow stronger in faith, knowing that He is with you through every struggle.

Journal Question: How can you allow God to use your failures as opportunities to grow in character, faith, and hope?

Weekly Summary

This week, we focused on dealing with failure by understanding that it's a normal part of life, learning from mistakes, accepting God's grace, moving forward, and turning failure into an opportunity for growth. God uses every experience — including failure — to shape you, teach you, and grow you into the person He's called you to be.

Real-Life Story

Walt Disney: Failure as a Stepping Stone to Success Early in his career, Disney faced numerous setbacks and challenges that could have derailed him. After moving to Hollywood in the 1920s, he launched a series of animation studios, but his first company, Laugh-O-Gram Studio, went bankrupt. Faced with failure, Disney had to start over, but he remained determined to pursue his passion for animation. In 1923, he and his brother Roy founded the Disney Brothers Studio, which later became The Walt Disney Company.

Despite his eventual success, Disney faced many obstacles along the way, including struggles with finances, creative disagreements, and the loss of his beloved character Oswald the Lucky Rabbit, who was taken from him by his distributor. However, instead of giving up, he created a new character—Mickey Mouse—who would go on to become an iconic figure in animation and entertainment. Reflecting on the value of failure in his life, Disney once said, "I think it's important to have a good hard failure when you're young. I learned a lot from that. I'm still learning" (Greene, 2016).

Throughout his career, Disney maintained a strong Christian faith, which provided him with hope and resilience during difficult times. His perseverance paid off as he revolutionized the animation industry and created beloved characters and theme parks that continue to bring joy to millions. Disney's journey is a testament to the idea that failure can lead to growth and unexpected success, inspiring countless people to pursue their dreams despite setbacks.

Prayer

"God, thank You for Your grace when I fail. Help me to see failure as an opportunity to learn, grow, and trust You more. Teach me to let go of my mistakes, to move forward in faith, and to use every experience as a way to become more like You. Amen."

BUILDING HEALTHY HABITS

Practical Challenge

Pick one habit you'd like to develop this week, whether it's praying daily, reading the Bible each morning, listening to a biblical podcast, or speaking more kindly to others. Create a simple plan to stay consistent in this habit, and ask God for strength to stick with it.

Day 1: How Small Habits Can Lead to Big Changes

Scripture: *Luke 16:10* - "'If you are faithful in little things, you will be faithful in large ones. But if you are dishonest in little things, you won't be honest with greater responsibilities." (NLT)

Reflection: The small habits you build today can lead to significant changes in your life. Whether it's spending time in prayer, being disciplined in schoolwork, or showing kindness to others, small actions add up over time. God honors faithfulness in the little things and uses them to build character and maturity in you. Don't underestimate the power of small, consistent habits that lead to big growth.

Journal Question: What small habits can you start today that will lead to big changes in your life and relationship with God?

Day 2: Developing Spiritual Habits Like Prayer and Bible Reading

Scripture: *Psalm 1:2-3* - "But they delight in the law of the Lord, meditating on it day and night. They are like trees planted along the riverbank, bearing fruit each season. Their leaves never wither, and they prosper in all they do." (NLT)

Reflection: Making a habit of spending time in God's Word and in prayer helps you grow in your relationship with Him. Just like a tree that stays strong and fruitful when planted by water, you become rooted and strengthened when you meditate on God's Word and connect with Him through prayer. Set a goal to make these spiritual habits part of your daily routine, and see how they transform your walk with God.

Journal Question: What are some daily routines you currently have, whether intentional or unintentional? Are there any of them that can be changed to better reflect the things that you most value spending your time on?

Day 3: Creating Routines That Honor God

Scripture: *1 Timothy 4:7-8* - "Do not waste time arguing over godless ideas and old wives' tales. Instead, train yourself to be godly. 'Physical training is good, but training for godliness is much better, promising benefits in this life and in the life to come.'" (NLT)

Reflection: Your routines and habits reflect what you value. When you create routines that honor God, like setting time aside for worship, serving others, or practicing gratitude, you're living in a way that brings Him glory and you're training yourself in godliness. Ask God to help you create routines that not only help you grow but also point others to Him. Let every part of your day — big or small — be an opportunity to honor God.

Journal Question: Where do you see the opportunity to create a routine of service and generosity in your life? This could be a daily, weekly, or even monthly routine of sharing your time and resources with someone who needs it as an act of training yourself in godliness.

Day 4: Breaking Bad Habits with God's Help

Scripture: *Colossians 3:8-10-* "But now is the time to get rid of anger, rage, malicious behavior, slander, and dirty language. Don't lie to each other, for you have stripped off your old sinful nature and all its wicked deeds. Put on your new nature, and be renewed as you learn to know your Creator and become like him." (NLT)

Reflection: Everyone has habits that need to be changed, whether it's speaking negatively, procrastinating, or giving in to temptation. Breaking bad habits can be hard, but God gives you the power to walk by the Spirit and make choices that align with His will. When you rely on God's strength and guidance, you can overcome bad habits and replace them with habits that bring life and honor to God.

Journal Question: What bad habits do you need God's help to break, and how can you rely on the Holy Spirit to overcome them?

Day 5: Staying Consistent in Building Healthy Habits

Scripture: *Hebrews 12:11* - "No discipline is enjoyable while it is happening—it's painful! But afterward there will be a peaceful harvest of right living for those who are trained in this way." (NLT)

Reflection: Building healthy habits requires consistency and discipline, and it's not always easy. But the effort is worth it, as it produces spiritual growth, maturity, and peace. When you're tempted to give up, remember the fruit that comes from staying consistent. Ask God for the strength to keep going, even when it's hard, and trust that He will reward your faithfulness.

Journal Question: Are there any good habits that you have attempted to develop and slacked off on? Are there any bad habits you have attempted to get rid of and fallen back into? Invite God into those processes and ask for His strength to start fresh each time you fail.

Weekly Summary

This week, we focused on building healthy habits by understanding the power of small changes, developing spiritual habits, creating God-honoring routines, breaking bad habits, and staying consistent. Developing habits that draw you closer to God and strengthen your character is a journey of daily choices that lead to lasting growth.

Real-Life Story

William Carey: Discipline and Perseverance in Daily Habits William Carey, known as the "father of modern missions," was a missionary to India who displayed great discipline and commitment to daily habits that helped him achieve his God-given purpose. He dedicated his life to translating the Bible into multiple Indian languages, often working tirelessly despite many setbacks and challenges. Carey once said, "Expect great things from God; attempt great things for God" (Carey, 1792). His life shows how small, consistent habits of prayer, study, and discipline led to significant impact and growth in God's kingdom. Carey's example encourages us to develop healthy habits that honor God and contribute to His purpose for our lives.

Prayer

"God, thank You for the opportunity to build habits that honor You. Help me to develop healthy habits that strengthen my relationship with You, and give me the discipline to stay consistent. Show me how to break any bad habits with Your help, and guide me as I create routines that glorify You. Amen."

SETTING GOALS WITH GOD IN MIND

Practical Challenge

Choose one goal to pray about this week, asking God for wisdom, direction, and timing. Write down small steps you can take toward achieving it, and be open to God's guidance and redirection along the way.

Day 1: Why It's Important to Set Goals That Align with God's Will

Scripture: *Proverbs 16:3* - "Commit to the Lord whatever you do, and he will establish your plans." (NIV)

Reflection: Setting goals is an important part of growth, but it's crucial to align your goals with God's will. When you commit your plans to the Lord, He guides and establishes them according to His purpose. Seek God's direction as you set goals for school, relationships, and spiritual growth, and trust that He will lead you toward His best for your life.

Journal Question: What are some goals you want to set, and how can you make sure they align with God's will?

Day 2: Praying About Your Goals and Dreams

Scripture: *Isaiah 28:29* - "All this also comes from the Lord Almighty, whose plan is wonderful, whose wisdom is magnificent." (NIV)

Reflection: God is the best counselor and guide when it comes to setting goals and achieving dreams! Which makes prayer an essential step in setting goals. Bring your dreams, desires, and plans before God in prayer and ask Him to give you wisdom and clarity. Don't be anxious about your future — instead, trust that God will guide you as you seek His will. When you pray about your goals, you're inviting God to be part of your journey and direction.

Journal Question: Have you ever seen God bring an opportunity to you that you were not expecting, and it turned out to be much better than what you had been imagining or planning? What was that experience like?

Day 3: Breaking Big Goals into Manageable Steps

Scripture: *Psalm 37:23* - "The Lord directs the steps of the godly. He delights in every detail of their lives." (NLT)

Reflection: Sometimes goals can seem overwhelming or impossible to achieve. Breaking them down into manageable steps helps you stay focused and make progress one step at a time. Trust that God will guide your steps as you delight in Him. Remember, it's not about reaching your goals all at once — it's about faithfully taking one step at a time toward the purpose God has placed on your heart.

Journal Question: What big goals can you break down into smaller, manageable steps to help you make progress?

Day 4: Trusting God's Timing for Your Goals

Scripture: *Ecclesiastes 3:11* - "Yet God has made everything beautiful for its own time. He has planted eternity in the human heart, but even so, people cannot see the whole scope of God's work from beginning to end." (NLT)

Reflection: God's timing is perfect, even if it doesn't match your expectations. There may be times when you set a goal and it doesn't happen right away, but trust that God is at work behind the scenes. He makes all things beautiful in their time, and He knows what's best for you. Be patient and trust that God will bring your goals to fulfillment according to His perfect timing as you take small steps of obedience each day.

Journal Question: Is there an area of your life where you feel like you aren't reaching your goals as quickly as you would like? Have a conversation with the Lord and reaffirm your trust in His timing.

Day 5: Being Flexible and Open to God's Redirection

Scripture: *James 4:13-15* - "Look here, you who say, 'Today or tomorrow we are going to a certain town and will stay there a year. We will do business there and make a profit.' How do you know what your life will be like tomorrow? Your life is like the morning fog—it's here a little while, then it's gone. What you ought to say is, 'If the Lord wants us to, we will live and do this or that.'" (NLT)

Reflection: It's great to set goals and make plans, but always remain flexible and open to God's redirection. Sometimes, God will lead you in a different direction than you expected, but His plans are always for your good. Be willing to adjust your goals if God shows you a new path, and trust that He knows what's best for your life.

Journal Question: Are you open to God's redirection in your life, and how can you be willing to adjust your goals as He leads?

Weekly Summary

This week, we explored setting goals with God in mind by aligning your goals with His will, praying for guidance, breaking down big goals, trusting God's timing, and staying flexible to His redirection. Setting goals is an important part of growth, but it's essential to keep God at the center and trust Him with every step.

Real-Life Story

David Green: Setting Goals with God's Purpose in Mind David Green, founder of Hobby Lobby, has built a successful business while keeping God at the center of his goals and decisions. Throughout his career, Green has remained committed to honoring God through his work and has sought God's guidance in every decision. He once said, "I just keep my eyes on Christ, and I try to keep my goals aligned with what He wants for my life" (Greene, 2017). Green's story is a reminder that when you set goals with God's purpose in mind, He will lead and bless your path.

Prayer

"God, thank You for giving me dreams and goals. Help me to set goals that align with Your will, to trust Your timing, and to stay flexible to Your leading. Guide my steps as I pursue the purpose You have for my life, and help me to keep You at the center of all my plans. Amen."

DEVELOPING A GRATEFUL HEART

Practical Challenge

Start a gratitude journal this week, writing down at least three things you're thankful for each day. Reflect on God's goodness, and let gratitude fill your heart, even in the midst of challenges.

Day 1: Keeping a Gratitude Journal to Remind Yourself of God's Goodness

Scripture: *Psalm 103:2* - "Let all that I am praise the Lord; may I never forget the good things he does for me." (NLT)

Reflection: Keeping a gratitude journal is a practical way to remember God's blessings. Write down the things you're thankful for each day — big or small. Over time, you'll be able to look back and see how God has been faithful, even in tough times. A heart of gratitude is constantly reminded of God's goodness and love, and it helps you stay encouraged in all seasons.

Journal Question: How might keeping a gratitude journal help you remember God's goodness and faithfulness?

Day 2: How to Focus on Blessings Instead of Problems

Scripture: *Psalm 107:1-2* - "Give thanks to the Lord, for he is good! His faithful love endures forever. Has the Lord redeemed you? Then speak out! Tell others he has redeemed you from your enemies." (NLT)

Reflection: Life will always have its share of problems, but choosing to focus on blessings brings joy and peace. When you find yourself overwhelmed by stress, anxiety, or frustration, pause and think about what God has blessed you with. Make a habit of focusing on things that are good, pure, and praiseworthy, and allow gratitude to bring positivity into your life.

Journal Question: Is there an area of your life where you have been focusing only on the problems you see? What are some blessings that you can name in that specific situation?

Day 3: The Importance of Gratitude in Daily Life

Scripture: *1 Thessalonians 5:18* - "Be thankful in all circumstances, for this is God's will for you who belong to Christ Jesus." (NLT)

Reflection: Gratitude is an attitude that God calls you to have in all situations. It's easy to be grateful when things are going well, but God also wants you to give thanks in difficult times. When you choose gratitude, it changes your perspective, helping you to focus on God's goodness rather than your problems. Each day, find reasons to thank God and see how it transforms your heart and attitude.

Journal Question: What are some things you're thankful for today? What can you do to make gratitude a daily habit?

Day 4: Learning to Give Thanks Even in Difficult Situations

Scripture: *1 Peter 4:12-13* - "Dear friends, don't be surprised at the fiery trials you are going through, as if something strange were happening to you. Instead, be very glad—for these trials make you partners with Christ in his suffering, so that you will have the wonderful joy of seeing his glory when it is revealed to all the world." (NLT)

Reflection: It may seem strange to give thanks during difficult situations, but God often uses trials to shape your character and grow your faith. When you choose gratitude in hard times, you're trusting God's purpose and believing that He is working for your good. Even in challenges, there are reasons to be thankful, knowing that God is with you and using every circumstance to help you grow.

Journal Question: What challenges are you facing right now and how can you choose to be grateful even in difficult situations?

Day 5: How Gratitude Brings Joy and Contentment

Scripture: *Colossians 3:15* - "And let the peace that comes from Christ rule in your hearts. For as members of one body you are called to live in peace. And always be thankful." (NLT)

Reflection: Gratitude leads to a life of joy and contentment. When you focus on what God has given you instead of what you lack, you find peace in His provision and joy in His presence. Let the peace of Christ fill your heart, and let gratitude overflow into every area of your life. A thankful heart is a joyful heart, and it brings contentment in all circumstances.

Journal Question: How have you seen gratitude bring joy and contentment to your life? How can you cultivate a more grateful heart?

Weekly Summary

This week, we explored developing a grateful heart by understanding the importance of daily gratitude, focusing on blessings, keeping a gratitude journal, giving thanks in difficult situations, and finding joy and contentment through gratitude. A heart filled with thankfulness transforms your perspective, brings peace, and helps you see God's faithfulness in every season.

Real-Life Story

Corrie Ten Boom: Gratitude in the Midst of Suffering Corrie ten Boom, a survivor of a Nazi concentration camp and author of *The Hiding Place*, understood the power of gratitude in difficult circumstances. She and her sister Betsie were imprisoned for hiding Jews during World War II, yet they chose to give thanks even while suffering. One day, they thanked God for the fleas infesting their barracks, only to later find out that the fleas kept the guards away, allowing them to hold Bible studies in secret. Corrie's life shows that gratitude can be found even in the darkest times, and God uses all things for His glory (Ten Boom, 1974).

Prayer

"God, thank You for Your goodness and faithfulness in my life. Help me to develop a grateful heart, to focus on my blessings instead of my problems, and to give thanks in all circumstances. Let my gratitude bring joy, peace, and contentment, and let it reflect Your love to those around me. Amen."

WEEK 33

MANAGING TIME WISELY

Practical Challenge

Make a list of all of your activities this week. Then go back and number those activities with a number between 1 and 5. 1 signifies that the activity has no importance in the Kingdom of God and 5 means the activity is very important in the Kingdom of God. After you complete this task, consider what things you can take out of your schedule to make God's Kingdom a higher priority as far as how you actually spend your time.

Day 1: The Importance of Using Your Time for God's Glory

Scripture: *Psalm 90:12* - "Teach us to realize the brevity of life, so that we may grow in wisdom." (NLT)

Reflection: Your time is a gift from God, and it's important to use it wisely for His glory. Life is short, and each day is an opportunity to live in a way that honors God and serves others. Ask God for wisdom in how you spend your time, and seek to make each day count for His kingdom. Remember that how you use your time reflects your priorities and values.

Journal Question: How can you use your time more effectively to bring glory to God and grow in your faith?

Day 2: Identifying Time-Wasters and Distractions

Scripture: *Romans 13:11* - "This is all the more urgent, for you know how late it is; time is running out. Wake up, for our salvation is nearer now than when we first believed." (NLT)

Reflection: It's easy to forget when you are young, but time is your most precious resource. It's the only resource you can never get more of or get back once it's gone. It's easy to get caught up in time-wasters and distractions that keep you from what's truly important. Identify the things in your life that pull you away from God's purpose, whether it's social media, video games, or unnecessary activities. Be wise with your time, and make the most of every opportunity to grow, serve, and honor God.

Journal Question: What are some distractions or time-wasters that you need to limit or remove from your life? What are the things in life that are actually worth you spending your most limited resource on: time?

Day 3: Learning to Prioritize Your Tasks

Scripture: *Isaiah 46:10* - "Only I can tell you the future before it even happens. Everything I plan will come to pass, for I do whatever I wish." (NLT)

Reflection: God is the only one who knows exactly what needs to be focused on at what time so that His perfect plans come to pass. Invite Him to help you prioritize your tasks and focus on what matters most each day. Put God first in all you do, and let Him direct how you spend your time. When your priorities align with God's will, you'll find that your time is used in meaningful and fruitful ways.

Journal Question: How can you prioritize your tasks each day to align with God's will and purpose?

Day 4: Making Time for Rest and Sabbath

Scripture: *Mark 2:27* - "Then Jesus said to them, 'The Sabbath was made to meet the needs of people, and not people to meet the requirements of the Sabbath.'" (NLT)

Reflection: God created rest as an important part of life. Taking time to rest and observe a Sabbath helps you recharge, reflect on God's goodness, and find peace in His presence. Managing your time wisely includes knowing when to work and when to rest. By setting aside time for rest, you honor God's design for balance and allow Him to refresh your body, mind, and spirit.

Journal Question: What areas of your life do you struggle to balance activity and rest; how can putting God first help you find that balance?

Day 5: Seeking God's Guidance on How to Use Your Time

Scripture: *Romans 11:33* - "Oh, how great are God's riches and wisdom and knowledge! How impossible it is for us to understand his decisions and his ways!" (NLT)

Reflection: When you're unsure of how to spend your time or feel overwhelmed by responsibilities, seek God's guidance. Ask Him for wisdom in how to use your time effectively, and trust that He will lead you. Let God's priorities become your priorities and allow His direction to shape your schedule, decisions, and activities.

Journal Question: How can you seek God's guidance and wisdom in managing your time and responsibilities?

Weekly Summary

This week, we focused on managing time wisely by using your time for God's glory, identifying time-wasters, prioritizing your tasks, balancing responsibilities, and seeking God's guidance. Your time is a gift from God, and how you use it makes a big difference in your growth, relationships, and impact for God's kingdom.

Real-Life Story

J.C. Penney: Using Time and Resources Wisely J.C. Penney, the founder of the J.C. Penney retail chain, was a businessman who understood the importance of managing time and resources with God's guidance. In the early days of his business, Penney faced the pressures of running his stores and meeting the demands of an expanding retail empire. He often found himself working long hours, sometimes at the expense of his health and family life. However, he realized that success in business should not come at the cost of neglecting his loved ones or his personal well-being.

One significant turning point came after he faced a severe health crisis in the 1930s, which forced him to reevaluate his life. He had experienced a series of personal and financial challenges, including the death of his beloved wife and the stress of the Great Depression affecting his business. During this tumultuous time, Penney began to focus on how he was spending his time, choosing to prioritize what truly mattered: his faith, family, and the well-being of his employees. He made a conscious decision to allocate his time to activities that aligned with his values, such as attending church, spending quality moments with family, and engaging with the community. He began to implement practices in his business that emphasized the importance of work-life balance, encouraging his employees to do the same.

J.C. Penney's transformation not only improved his personal life but also positively influenced his business practices. He fostered a company culture that valued integrity, respect, and a commitment to service, which resonated with both his employees and customers. Ultimately, Penney's decision to prioritize his time wisely led to a legacy that went beyond retail success; it demonstrated the importance of living a balanced life centered on core values and meaningful relationships. His story continues to inspire many in both business and personal realms, reminding us that true success involves wise stewardship of our time and resources (Jones, 1971).

Prayer

"God, thank You for the gift of time. Help me to use it wisely, to balance my responsibilities, and to seek Your guidance in all I do. Show me how to prioritize my tasks, limit distractions, and make the most of every opportunity to grow in You and serve others. Amen."

STAYING HUMBLE

Practical Challenge

Find a way to serve someone this week in humility, whether it's helping a friend, volunteering, or simply showing kindness to someone in need. Let your act of service be an expression of Christ's love and humility.

Day 1: Why Humility Is a Key Christian Virtue

Scripture: *Philippians 2:3-4* - "Don't be selfish; don't try to impress others. Be humble, thinking of others as better than yourselves. Don't look out only for your own interests, but take an interest in others, too." (NLT)

Reflection: Humility is the opposite of pride. It's about valuing others and putting their needs above your own. Jesus set the perfect example of humility, and He calls you to follow in His steps. True humility isn't about putting yourself down — it's about lifting others up and being willing to serve. As you grow in humility, you reflect Christ's character and bring glory to God.

Journal Question: What does humility mean to you, and how can you grow in it?

Day 2: How Jesus Demonstrated Humility

Scripture: *John 13:14-15* - "And since I, your Lord and Teacher, have washed your feet, you ought to wash each other's feet. I have given you an example to follow. Do as I have done to you." (NLT)

Reflection: Jesus, the Son of God, demonstrated ultimate humility when He washed His disciples' feet, an act normally reserved for the lowest servant. By serving others with love and humility, Jesus showed what true greatness looks like. Humility is not about seeking recognition or status — it's about being willing to serve and love others as Jesus did. Follow His example and find joy in putting others before yourself.

Journal Question: How can following Jesus' example of service help you live a more humble life?

Day 3: Recognizing Your Strengths Without Becoming Proud

Scripture: *Romans 12:3* - "Because of the privilege and authority God has given me, I give each of you this warning: Don't think you are better than you really are. Be honest in your evaluation of yourselves, measuring yourselves by the faith God has given us." (NLT)

Reflection: Humility doesn't mean denying your strengths and talents; it means recognizing them as gifts from God. Be confident in who God made you to be. But stay grounded, and give Him the credit for your abilities. Remember that every strength you have is an opportunity to serve others and honor God, not to build up your own pride. Let your gifts be a reflection of God's grace.

Journal Question: What are your strengths, and how can you use them to serve others while giving glory to God?

Day 4: Serving Others as an Act of Humility

Scripture: *Mark 10:45* - "For even the Son of Man came not to be served but to serve others and to give his life as a ransom for many.'" (NLT)

Reflection: One of the best ways to grow in humility is to serve others. When you choose to serve without expecting anything in return, you reflect the heart of Jesus, who came to serve rather than be served. Find opportunities to help those in need, support your friends, and show kindness to strangers. Let your service be an act of humility that points others to the love of Christ.

Journal Question: How can you practice humility through serving others in your family, school, or community?

Day 5: How to Accept Praise Without Letting It Inflate Your Ego

Scripture: *1 Corinthians 1:31* - "Therefore, as the Scriptures say, 'If you want to boast, boast only about the Lord.'" (NLT)

Reflection: When others praise or compliment you, it can be easy to let it go to your head. But humility means accepting praise with grace while giving the glory back to God. When someone recognizes your achievements or strengths, thank them sincerely and use it as an opportunity to praise God for His goodness in your life. Let any praise you receive point back to the One who gave you the gifts and talents you have.

Journal Question: When you receive praise or recognition, how can you respond in a way that reflects humility and honors God?

Weekly Summary

This week, we focused on staying humble by understanding the importance of humility as a Christian virtue, following Jesus' example, recognizing your strengths without pride, serving others, and learning to accept praise without letting it inflate your ego. Humility is a path to reflecting Christ's love and character to the world, and it leads to deeper relationships and greater joy.

Real-Life Story

Billy Graham: A Humble Heart for God Billy Graham, one of the most well-known evangelists in history, was known not just for his preaching but also for his humility. Despite speaking to millions of people around the world, Graham always pointed the glory back to God. After one of his sermons, a prominent Hollywood producer approached him with an offer to film his crusades, which would significantly elevate his visibility and potentially lead to greater success. However, Graham was cautious and wanted to ensure that the focus remained on the message of Christ, not on himself. He politely declined the offer, feeling that it would detract from the gospel's central message.

Later, Graham was invited to meet with the producer and other influential figures in the entertainment industry. Instead of entering with an air of self-importance, he chose to approach the meeting with humility. He shared about his own shortcomings, how he was just a simple preacher called by God, and how his desire was to lead people to Christ rather than to gain fame or recognition. This humility resonated with those present, leaving a lasting impression on many who were used to the spotlight. Graham's approach not only exemplified his commitment to serving God above personal ambition but also helped build relationships with those who might have otherwise felt disconnected from the church.

Through moments like these, Billy Graham consistently demonstrated that true greatness comes from serving others and that humility is key to being an effective servant of Christ. His life remains a testament to the power of humility in leadership and ministry. He once said, "The ground is level at the foot of the cross, and I am just one of many who have been saved by God's grace" (Graham, 2006).

His humble heart and focus on serving others made a lasting impact, and his life is a powerful reminder that humility leads to greatness in God's kingdom.

Prayer

"God, thank You for showing me what true humility looks like through Jesus. Help me to grow in humility, to serve others with love, and to use my strengths for Your glory. Teach me to accept praise without pride and to live in a way that reflects Your love and grace to those around me. Amen."

WEEK 35

HONORING YOUR PARENTS

Practical Challenge

Choose one practical way to serve or appreciate your parents this week. Whether it's helping out around the house, writing a note of thanks, or spending quality time with them, find a way to honor them through your actions.

Day 1: Understanding the Biblical Command to Honor Parents

Scripture: *Ephesians 6:2-3* - "'Honor your father and mother.' This is the first commandment with a promise: If you honor your father and mother, 'things will go well for you, and you will have a long life on the earth.'" (NLT)

Reflection: Honoring your parents is a command given by God with a promise of blessing. It means showing respect, love, and obedience to them as they guide you. This command isn't just about following rules but recognizing the importance of family relationships and the wisdom they provide.

Even when it's difficult, honoring your parents brings joy to God's heart and blessings to your life.

Journal Question: What are some specific ways you can honor your parents in your daily life?

Day 2: Showing Respect Even When You Disagree

Scripture: *Colossians 3:20* - "Children, always obey your parents, for this pleases the Lord." (NLT)

Reflection: It's natural to have disagreements with your parents, especially as you grow older and develop your own thoughts and opinions. However, God calls us to respect and honor our parents even in times of conflict. It's possible to disagree respectfully, listening to their perspective and speaking with kindness. Remember that honoring your parents doesn't mean you'll always see eye to eye, but it means valuing and respecting them regardless.

Journal Question: How do you handle disagreements with your parents, and how can you show respect even when you disagree?

Day 3: Practical Ways to Serve and Appreciate Your Parents

Scripture: *Proverbs 23:22* - "Listen to your father, who gave you life, and do not despise your mother when she is old." (NIV)

Reflection: Honoring your parents is more than words — it's shown through actions. Small acts of service, like helping with chores, saying thank you, and showing appreciation, communicate love and respect. Taking time to listen to their advice and caring for their needs are ways to honor the role they play in your life. Look for ways this week to serve and show appreciation to your parents.

Journal Question: What is one act of service or appreciation you can do this week to honor your parents?

Day 4: How Honoring Your Parents Honors God

Scripture: *Proverbs 1:8* - "My child, listen when your father corrects you. Don't neglect your mother's instruction." (NLT)

Reflection: Honoring your parents is one way of honoring God. They are placed in your life to guide, teach, and help you grow. When you choose to listen, respect, and follow their guidance, you are not only honoring them but also showing obedience to God. Trust that God sees your heart in how you treat your parents and that honoring them is an act of worship to Him.

Journal Question: How does knowing that honoring your parents honors God change your perspective on your relationship with them?

Day 5: Balancing Independence with Respect as You Grow

Scripture: *1 Timothy 5:4* - "But if she has children or grandchildren, their first responsibility is to show godliness at home and repay their parents by taking care of them. This is something that pleases God." (NLT)

Reflection: As you grow older, you gain more independence and make more decisions on your own. However, respecting your parents doesn't end when you leave home or become an adult. It's a lifelong commitment to value their influence and honor their place in your life. Balance independence with continued love and respect, recognizing that honoring your parents is a way to show love to God as well.

Journal Question: As you gain more independence, what steps can you take to continue showing love and respect to your parents? Who are some adults in your life that you see setting a good example of what it looks like to continue honoring their parents even long beyond living in their parents' home?

Weekly Summary

This week, we explored what it means to honor your parents, even in disagreements. We looked at practical ways to serve and show appreciation and learned how honoring your parents is also a way of honoring God. Balancing independence with respect is important as you grow, and finding ways to continually honor your parents brings joy to God.

Real-Life Story

Jim Elliot: Honoring Parents Through Life's Decisions Jim and Elisabeth Elliot were missionaries who served God faithfully in South America. Before they got married, Jim had to make a difficult decision — whether to obey

God's call to missions or stay with his family, who were concerned for his safety. Jim valued his parents' input and sought to maintain open lines of communication. Rather than rebelling against their wishes, he took the time to explain his passion for missions and the call he felt from God. Jim also demonstrated his respect by considering their perspective and acknowledging their fears. Ultimately, Jim did follow the Lord's call and went into missions in South America; however, He continued to engage with his parents, showing them that he was making an informed and prayerful decision. His respectful approach reflected both his love for them and his dedication to his faith, highlighting the balance he sought between honoring his parents and following the Lord's calling. Even on the mission field later in life, both Jim and Elisabeth continued to honor their parents by sharing their journeys with them, praying for them, and valuing their wisdom (Elliot, 1989, *Shadow of the Almighty*).

Prayer

"Dear God, thank You for my parents and the role they play in my life. Help me to honor, respect, and love them in all I do. Give me wisdom in times of disagreement and show me ways to serve and appreciate them each day. Let my relationship with my parents honor You. Amen."

RESPECTING AUTHORITY

Practical Challenge

This week, choose one authority figure in your life to show appreciation and respect for. It could be your teacher, coach, pastor, or another leader. Write them a note, say thank you, or find a way to express your gratitude for their leadership.

Day 1: Why God Calls Us to Respect Authority Figures

Scripture: *Romans 13:1* - "Everyone must submit to governing authorities. For all authority comes from God, and those in positions of authority have been placed there by God." (NLT)

Reflection: God calls us to respect and submit to the authority figures He has placed in our lives — whether parents, teachers, coaches, or government leaders. When we show respect, we are not just honoring them but also honoring God's design for order and leadership. Even when we don't fully agree, we can show respect by being willing to listen and respond in love.

Journal Question: How do you already show respect to the authority figures in your life, and where can you improve?

Day 2: The Role of Teachers, Coaches, and Leaders in Your Life

Scripture: *Hebrews 13:17* - "Have confidence in your leaders and submit to their authority, because they keep watch over you as those who must give an account. Do this so that their work will be a joy, not a burden, for that would be of no benefit to you." (NIV)

Reflection: Teachers, coaches, pastors, and leaders are in your life to guide you, teach you, and help you grow. Respecting their role means being willing to listen, learn, and follow their guidance, or find ways to respectfully disagree with them when needed. When you show respect to those in authority, you honor God's design and recognize His authority in placing people in roles of leadership in your life. God will hold them accountable for every decision they make that affects the people under their leadership; they have a hard job! Think about how you can show appreciation and respect for the leaders God has placed in your life.

Journal Question: Think of an authority figure you respect. What qualities do you appreciate in them? Why?

Day 3: How to Respectfully Disagree with Authority

Scripture: *Proverbs 15:1* - "A gentle answer turns away wrath, but a harsh word stirs up anger." (NIV)

Reflection: There may be times when you don't agree with an authority figure in your life, and that's okay. Disagreement doesn't have to mean disrespect. You can voice your thoughts in a calm and respectful manner, being careful to speak kindly and listen well. Approaching disagreements with a gentle and humble heart helps build understanding and shows honor to the person in authority. It may be that if you listen carefully, they will help you understand a viewpoint you had not seen before. Or it may be that you will agree to disagree at the end of the conversation, but either way, approaching the disagreement with humility and respect will lead to a better conclusion.

Journal Question: Think of a time when you disagreed with someone in authority. How did you handle it, and what could you do differently next time?

Day 4: The Importance of Submitting to Authority When Appropriate

Scripture: *Titus 3:1* - "Remind the people to be subject to rulers and authorities, to be obedient, to be ready to do whatever is good," (NIV)

Reflection: Submission isn't about blindly following anyone in authority; it's about recognizing that God has placed leaders in our lives for our good. When we submit to their leadership — whether in school, sports, church, or other areas — we learn discipline, humility, and respect. Submission is an act of obedience to God and helps create peace and order in our lives.

Journal Question: Why is it important to submit to authority, and how does submission reflect your obedience to God?

Day 5: When to Seek Help if Authority is Abusive or Wrong

Scripture: *Matthew 7:15-20* - "'Beware of false prophets who come disguised as harmless sheep but are really vicious wolves. You can identify them by their fruit, that is, by the way they act. Can you pick grapes from thornbushes, or figs from thistles? A good tree produces good fruit, and a bad tree produces bad fruit. A good tree can't produce bad fruit, and a bad tree can't produce good fruit. So every tree that does not produce good fruit is chopped down and thrown into the fire. Yes, just as you can identify a tree by its fruit, so you can identify people by their actions.'" (NLT)

Reflection: While God calls us to respect and submit to authority, it's important to know that abuse of power or wrongdoing should not be ignored. If an authority figure is acting in a way that harms or abuses you or others, it's crucial to seek help from a trusted adult, pastor, or counselor. God does not condone abuse, and He desires justice, protection, and care for those who are vulnerable. Don't stay quiet if you are experiencing or witnessing injustice or abuse.

Journal Question: If you've ever experienced or witnessed authority being used abusively, how did you respond, and who did you turn to for help? Is there something you would do differently if you faced a situation like that again?

Weekly Summary

This week, we learned about respecting authority and why God has placed leaders in our lives. Whether it's teachers, coaches, or government leaders, respecting authority is a way to honor God. We also explored how to disagree respectfully, submit appropriately, and seek help if authority is misused. Building a culture of respect helps us live in harmony and reflect God's heart for leadership.

Real-Life Story

Dietrich Bonhoeffer: Respecting Authority with Courage Dietrich Bonhoeffer was a German pastor and theologian during World War II who respected authority but was also willing to stand up for what was right. In the early 1930s, as Hitler's government began to impose oppressive policies, Bonhoeffer was deeply troubled by the church's complicity in these actions. Many church leaders were either silent or supportive of the regime, but Bonhoeffer believed that Christians had a moral obligation to oppose evil.

In 1934, he attended a meeting of the German Evangelical Church, where discussions about the Nazi influence on the church were taking place. During the meeting, Bonhoeffer courageously spoke out against the state's encroachment into church affairs and the moral compromises that many church leaders were making. He respectfully confronted his colleagues, urging them to recognize the dangers of aligning with the Nazi government.

He famously said, "Silence in the face of evil is itself evil. God will not hold us guiltless. Not to speak is to speak. Not to act is to act" (Bonhoeffer, 2001). This quote encapsulated his conviction that Christians could not remain passive in the face of injustice.

Despite the risk of backlash from those in power, Bonhoeffer continued to advocate for the church to stand firm in its principles. He became involved in the Confessing Church movement, which sought to maintain the integrity of the Christian faith against Nazi ideology. As the situation in Germany worsened, Bonhoeffer's resistance intensified. Ultimately, Bonhoeffer was arrested in 1943 and executed in a concentration camp in 1945 for his opposition to the Nazi regime. His legacy as a courageous voice against tyranny and his refusal to remain silent in the face of evil continues to inspire people around the world to stand up for justice and truth (Metaxas, 2010).

Prayer

"God, thank You for the leaders and authority figures You've placed in my life. Help me to show them respect and honor, and give me wisdom to handle disagreements with grace. Teach me to submit to authority when appropriate and to stand for truth when necessary. Amen."

Week 37

Choosing the Right Friends

Practical Challenge

Reach out to a friend who has been a positive influence in your life. Thank them for their friendship and encourage them in their faith. Make time to spend together, pray together, or simply catch up and support one another.

Day 1: How Friends Influence Your Decisions and Character

Scripture: *Proverbs 13:20* - "Walk with the wise and become wise, for a companion of fools suffers harm." (NIV)

Reflection: Friends have a powerful influence on who we are and who we become. The people you choose to spend time with can either push you closer to God or pull you away from Him. Surrounding yourself with wise and encouraging friends helps you grow in your character and faith, while negative influences can lead you to make poor choices. Be intentional about who you walk with.

Journal Question: Who are the friends in your life that encourage your faith and character development? How can you spend more time with them?

Day 2: What Makes a Friendship Healthy and Godly

Scripture: *Proverbs 18:24* - "There are 'friends' who destroy each other, but a real friend sticks closer than a brother." (NLT)

Reflection: A healthy, godly friendship is one where both people encourage each other to grow in faith, help each other through struggles, and share a deep sense of love and respect. Godly friends challenge you to be your best, lift you up when you're down, and point you toward Christ. Seek friendships that are mutually supportive, loving, and centered on God.

Journal Question: What qualities do you think are important in a godly friend, and how can you seek those qualities in your own friendships?

Day 3: Signs of Toxic Friendships to Avoid

Scripture: *1 Corinthians 15:33* - "Do not be deceived: 'Evil company corrupts good habits.'" (NKJV)

Reflection: Some friendships can harm your faith and lead you down the wrong path. Toxic friends may constantly criticize, gossip, pressure you to make poor choices, or lead you away from God. It's important to recognize these unhealthy relationships and set boundaries. Choose friends who encourage your growth in Christ rather than those who draw you away from Him.

Journal Question: Are there any friendships that have a negative influence on your relationship with God? How can you set healthy boundaries?

Day 4: The Value of Having Christian Friends

Scripture: *Hebrews 10:24-25* - "And let us consider how we may spur one another on toward love and good deeds, not giving up meeting together, as some are in the habit of doing, but encouraging one another—and all the more as you see the Day approaching." (NIV)

Reflection: Having Christian friends who share your faith is valuable for spiritual growth and encouragement. They understand your beliefs and can help you stay strong when facing challenges. Gathering together with Christian friends for prayer, encouragement, and accountability helps you grow closer to God and stay committed to living for Him.

Journal Question: How have your Christian friends helped you grow in your faith, and what are some ways you can encourage them in return?

Day 5: How to Be a Good Friend to Others

Scripture: *Proverbs 27:6* - "Wounds from a sincere friend are better than many kisses from an enemy." (NLT)

Reflection: Being a good friend to someone else does not mean always agreeing with them or always supporting their decisions. If you really care about someone in your life, you should lovingly encourage them to make better choices if they are choosing things that are unwise. Be faithful and stand by them in good times and in hard times, but be honest with them all the time. Support them in their walk with the Lord and encourage their growth.

Journal Question: How can you be a better friend to those around you, showing God's love and support?

Weekly Summary

This week, we explored how the friends we choose affect our decisions and character. We learned the qualities of a healthy and godly friendship, how to avoid toxic relationships, and the value of having Christian friends. Being a good friend means showing love, support, and encouragement, just as God shows His love to us.

Real-Life Story

William Wilberforce and John Newton: Friendship That Endured Adversity One famous Christian whose life was profoundly impacted by a friend's encouragement is William Wilberforce, the British politician and social reformer known for his tireless efforts to abolish the slave trade in England. His journey toward faith and perseverance in the face of immense difficulty was greatly influenced by his close friendship with John Newton, the former slave ship captain who became a prominent pastor and abolitionist.

Wilberforce experienced a spiritual awakening in the late 1770s, a time when he was grappling with his purpose in life and the moral implications of his political career. During this period, he sought guidance and support from Newton, who had once been involved in the slave trade himself but later found redemption through faith in Christ. Newton became a mentor and friend to Wilberforce, encouraging him to deepen his relationship with God and to consider the moral implications of his actions in the political sphere. Despite facing significant opposition and ridicule from those who profited from the slave trade, Wilberforce remained committed to the cause of abolition. Newton's wisdom and encouragement provided him with the spiritual fortitude to persevere through the challenges he encountered. Newton often reminded Wilberforce of the importance of faith and obedience to God's calling, emphasizing that true Christians are called to stand up against injustice.

Throughout the years, Wilberforce's resolve grew stronger, and he tirelessly campaigned for the abolition of slavery, introducing bills in Parliament and rallying public support. His faith and commitment were unwavering, fueled by the encouragement and friendship of John Newton. In 1807, after years of struggle, the British Parliament finally passed the Abolition of the Slave Trade Act. Wilberforce's legacy as a champion for justice and human rights is a testament to the impact that a faithful friend can have on one's life. His story demonstrates how encouragement, accountability, and the sharing of faith can lead to transformative action, even in the face of daunting obstacles (Metaxas, 2007).

Prayer

"Lord, thank You for the gift of friendship. Help me to choose friends who encourage me to grow in You, and give me the strength to be a godly friend to others. Show me how to set healthy boundaries and be a light in all of my relationships. Amen."

BUILDING HEALTHY FRIENDSHIPS

Practical Challenge

Plan to spend intentional time with a friend this week. Whether it's meeting up to play disc golf, going for a hike, or praying together, make time to connect, share, and grow in your friendship.

Day 1: Communicating Openly and Honestly with Friends

Scripture: *Ephesians 4:24-25* - "Put on your new nature, created to be like God—truly righteous and holy. So stop telling lies. Let us tell our neighbors the truth, for we are all parts of the same body." (NLT)

Reflection: Honest communication is key to any healthy friendship. It means being willing to share openly and listen attentively. Speaking the truth in love helps your friends grow and encourages deeper, more meaningful relationships. Honest conversations can sometimes be hard, but they build trust and understanding and create more meaningful relationships with others.

Journal Question: How can you improve your communication with your friends, being more open and honest?

Day 2: Supporting Each Other Through Good and Bad Times

Scripture: *Galatians 6:2* - "Carry each other's burdens, and in this way you will fulfill the law of Christ." (NIV)

Reflection: Good friends are there for each other in all seasons — whether life is going well or you're facing struggles. Supporting each other through good times brings joy, and carrying each other's burdens through bad times brings strength. Be willing to listen, pray, and stand with your friends in every situation, reflecting God's love and care.

Journal Question: What are some ways you can better support your friends in their struggles and in their joys?

Day 3: Encouraging Spiritual Growth in Your Friendships

Scripture: *1 Thessalonians 5:11* - "So encourage each other and build each other up, just as you are already doing." (NLT)

Reflection: Friendships are a place where spiritual growth can flourish. Encourage each other to read the Bible, pray, and live out your faith. When friends share their struggles, remind them of God's promises and help them stay rooted in Him. A friendship centered on God is one where both people inspire each other to grow closer to Him.

Journal Question: How can you encourage your friends to grow spiritually and draw closer to God?

Day 4: Setting Boundaries in Friendships

Scripture: *Proverbs 25:17* - "Seldom set foot in your neighbor's house, lest he become weary of you and hate you." (NKJV)

Reflection: Healthy friendships require boundaries. While it's great to be close to your friends, it's also important to respect each other's space, time, and privacy. Setting boundaries helps maintain balance and prevents misunderstandings or dependency. Be mindful of each other's needs and be willing to communicate clearly about boundaries.

Journal Question: Are there any boundaries you need to set in your friendships to keep them healthy? How can you communicate those boundaries with love?

Day 5: Making Time for Important Friendships

Scripture: *John 15:12-13* - "This is my commandment: Love each other in the same way I have loved you. There is no greater love than to lay down one's life for one's friends." (NLT)

Reflection: Good friendships require time and effort. Making time for the friends who encourage, support, and build you up is important. Nurturing these relationships helps them grow stronger and more meaningful. Be intentional about spending quality time with your friends, investing in the relationships that matter most.

Journal Question: What steps can you take to make more time for the friendships that matter most to you?

Weekly Summary

This week, we focused on building healthy friendships through open communication, supporting one another, encouraging spiritual growth, setting boundaries, and making time for important relationships. Godly friendships require effort, love, and understanding, and when cultivated well, they can be some of the most life-giving relationships you'll experience.

Real-Life Story

William Carey and Andrew Fuller: The Power of Godly Friendships
William Carey was a British shoemaker and a keen botanist who felt a calling to share the gospel in India. However, his journey was not easy, and it was the encouragement and support of his friend, Andrew Fuller, that helped sustain him during difficult times.

In the late 18th century, Carey faced skepticism and resistance from his contemporaries in England when he first proposed the idea of overseas missionary work. Many doubted the feasibility of his plans and the importance of reaching distant lands. Despite this, Carey persevered, driven by his deep faith and conviction. During this challenging period, Andrew Fuller became a significant source of encouragement for Carey. Fuller, a Baptist pastor and theologian, believed in Carey's vision and saw the importance of missions. He supported Carey both spiritually and practically, even helping to establish the Baptist Missionary Society in 1792, which sent Carey to India and financially supported him.

When Carey arrived in India in 1793, he faced numerous obstacles, including cultural differences, language barriers, and personal hardships. His early years were marked by struggle, including the death of his wife, Dorothy, and the challenges of establishing a mission in a foreign land. Throughout these trials, Carey often turned to Fuller for encouragement and guidance. Fuller's unwavering belief in Carey's mission helped bolster his spirits during these dark times. Carey's faith and perseverance ultimately led to remarkable achievements in India, including the translation of the Bible into several Indian languages and the establishment of educational institutions. His work laid the foundation for future missionary efforts and demonstrated the power of faith, obedience, and the support of friends in overcoming adversity. William Carey's relationship with Andrew Fuller exemplifies how encouragement and friendship can profoundly impact one's faith journey, especially during times of difficulty and doubt (Piper, 2016).

Prayer

"Lord, thank You for the gift of friendships that build me up and bring me closer to You. Help me to communicate openly, support others, encourage spiritual growth, and set healthy boundaries in my relationships. Let my friendships be filled with Your love, grace, and truth. Amen."

PEER PRESSURE

Practical Challenge

This week, identify an area of your life where you face peer pressure and practice saying "no." Whether it's pressure to talk a certain way, act in a way that doesn't reflect your faith, or compromise your values, stand firm and choose God's way over the world's way.

Day 1: Recognizing the Different Forms of Peer Pressure

Scripture: *Proverbs 1:10* - "My son, if sinful men entice you, do not give in to them." (NIV)

Reflection: Peer pressure can come in many forms — from friends, social media, or even the desire to fit in. Sometimes, it's direct, like someone urging you to do something wrong. Other times, it's subtle, like feeling the need to change who you are to be accepted. Recognizing when peer pressure is influencing you is the first step in standing firm in your faith.

Journal Question: What are some situations where you have felt peer pressure? How did you handle them?

Day 2: The Importance of Standing Up for What You Believe

Scripture: *1 Corinthians 16:13* - "Be on your guard; stand firm in the faith; be courageous; be strong." (NIV)

Reflection: It's not always easy to stand up for what you believe, especially when others are pushing you to go against your values. But God calls you to be courageous and stand firm in your faith. When you stand up for what's right, you set an example for others and show that God's approval is more important than fitting in with the crowd.

Journal Question: How can you stand firm in your beliefs when faced with pressure to do something against your values?

Day 3: Strategies for Saying "No" to Negative Influences

Scripture: *James 4:7* - "Therefore submit to God. Resist the devil and he will flee from you." (NKJV)

Reflection: Learning how to say "no" is an important skill when facing peer pressure. It takes courage to resist negative influences, but God gives you strength to stand your ground. Practice responding with confidence and clarity when someone tries to pressure you into doing something that goes against your faith or values.

Journal Question: What are some practical ways you can say "no" to negative influences in your life?

Day 4: Surrounding Yourself with People Who Support Your Values

Scripture: *1 Samuel 14:7* - "'Do all that you have in mind,' his armor-bearer said. 'Go ahead; I am with you heart and soul.'" (NIV)

Reflection: The people you spend time with have a huge influence on your decisions and character. Surround yourself with friends who support your values and encourage you to live for God. Good friends encourage you to obey God, helping you grow in faith and resist negative peer pressure.

Journal Question: Who are the friends that support your faith and encourage you to make wise decisions?

Day 5: How to Lead Others Instead of Following the Crowd

Scripture: *1 Peter 4:4-5* - "Of course, your former friends are surprised when you no longer plunge into the flood of wild and destructive things they do. So they slander you. But remember that they will have to face God, who stands ready to judge everyone, both the living and the dead." (NLT)

Reflection: God calls you to be a leader, not a follower of the world. Leading others means setting an example through your words and actions, and choosing to do what's right even when it's unpopular. By staying true to who God created you to be, you can influence others positively instead of being swayed by the crowd.

Journal Question: How can you be a leader who influences others in a positive way, instead of following the crowd?

Weekly Summary

This week, we discussed peer pressure and how to recognize it in its many forms. We learned the importance of standing up for what you believe, saying "no" to negative influences, surrounding yourself with supportive friends, and leading others instead of following the crowd. By staying grounded in your faith, you can overcome peer pressure and be a light to those around you.

Real-Life Story

Sadie Robertson Huff: Standing Firm in Faith A contemporary Christian who has stood firm in their faith amidst significant peer pressure is Sadie Robertson Huff, a well-known speaker, author, and former star of the reality TV show *Duck Dynasty*. During her teenage years, Sadie experienced intense pressure to conform to the expectations of her peers, especially regarding popularity and lifestyle choices. As she gained fame through the reality show, she found herself in situations where she was often faced with choices that conflicted with her Christian values.

One notable moment came during her high school years when Sadie was invited to attend parties and events where drinking and other risky behaviors were common. Many of her friends were engaging in activities that did not align with her beliefs, and she felt the weight of wanting to fit in while also wanting to honor her faith. In the midst of this pressure, Sadie leaned on her Christian upbringing and the teachings of her family. She chose to be open about her faith, sharing her convictions with her friends, which sometimes led to uncomfortable conversations. Instead of compromising her values, she decided to focus on being a positive influence, encouraging her peers to consider the choices they were making.

Sadie often spoke about the importance of surrounding herself with friends who shared her values and supported her faith journey. She made it clear that her identity was rooted in Christ and that she wanted to be a light in the darkness, even if it meant standing alone at times. This commitment resonated with many of her peers, leading some to respect her choices and even ask her for guidance. Her experiences ultimately shaped her into a strong advocate for living authentically as a Christian, encouraging others to embrace their faith without fear of judgment or rejection. Today, Sadie continues to use her platform to inspire young people to stand firm in their beliefs, demonstrating that it is possible to remain true to one's faith despite societal pressures (Huff, 2020).

Prayer

"God, help me to recognize peer pressure and give me the strength to stand firm in my faith. Surround me with friends who encourage me and help me to be a leader who influences others for good. Teach me to say 'no' to the world's way and 'yes' to Your way. Amen."

HOW TO BE A LEADER AMONG FRIENDS

Practical Challenge

Identify one area in your life where you can be a leader this week. Whether it's setting a good example, encouraging a friend, or standing up for what's right, step out in faith and lead others with integrity and love.

Day 1: Leading by Example with Integrity

Scripture: *1 Timothy 4:12* - "Don't let anyone think less of you because you are young. Be an example to all believers in what you say, in the way you live, in your love, your faith, and your purity." (NLT)

Reflection: Leadership isn't just about having a title — it's about setting an example. Your words, actions, and attitude speak louder than anything you say. When you lead with integrity and live out your faith, others are inspired to follow. Don't wait to be older or have a position of leadership; lead by example right where you are.

Journal Question: How can you lead by example in your words, actions, and attitude this week?

Day 2: Being a Positive Influence Without Being Controlling

Scripture: *1 Peter 2:12* - "Be careful to live properly among your unbelieving neighbors. Then even if they accuse you of doing wrong, they will see your honorable behavior, and they will give honor to God when he judges the world." (NLT)

Reflection: Leadership is about influence, not control. Being a positive influence means encouraging others to do what's right and inspiring them by how you live. It's not about making others do what you want, but about pointing them toward God and setting a good example. Shine your light in a way that leads others to see God's goodness.

Journal Question: What are some ways you can be a positive influence on people in your life without trying to control them?

Day 3: Encouraging Your Friends to Make Good Decisions

Scripture: *Hebrews 3:13* - "But encourage one another daily, as long as it is called 'Today,' so that none of you may be hardened by sin's deceitfulness." (NIV)

Reflection: One way to be a leader among your friends is to encourage them to make good choices. Offer positive words, pray for them, and be a voice of truth when they are struggling. God can use your encouragement to strengthen your friends' faith and help them make decisions that honor Him.

Journal Question: How can you encourage your friends to make decisions that honor God?

Day 4: Building Confidence as a Leader

Scripture: *Ephesians 6:10* - "A final word: Be strong in the Lord and in his mighty power." (NKJV)

Reflection: Being a leader takes confidence, but that confidence doesn't come from your own strength — it comes from knowing that God is with you. God calls you to be strong and courageous as you lead others. Step out in faith, trust that God will guide you, and lead with boldness, knowing that He is with you every step of the way.

Journal Question: What areas of your life do you need to step out in confidence and lead with boldness?

Day 5: Knowing When to Follow and When to Lead

Scripture: *Matthew 20:26-28* - "But among you it will be different. Whoever wants to be a leader among you must be your servant, and whoever wants to be first among you must become your slave. For even the Son of Man came not to be served but to serve others and to give his life as a ransom for many." (NLT)

Reflection: A good leader knows when to lead and when to follow. Humility is key in leadership — being willing to serve, listen, and let others take the lead when appropriate. True leadership is not about always being in charge, but about serving others and doing what's best for the group. It's about building others up and empowering them to reach their fullest potential.

Journal Question: Are there any areas of your life where practicing humility and letting someone else take the lead would actually be the best way to lead by example?

Weekly Summary

This week, we explored how to be a leader among your friends. Leading by example, being a positive influence, encouraging good decisions, and building confidence are all part of godly leadership. We also learned the importance of humility in knowing when to lead and when to follow. God calls you to be a leader who reflects His love and truth in all you do.

Real-Life Story

Truett Cathy: Leading Through Service Truett Cathy, the founder of Chick-fil-A, is a successful leader who embodies Jesus' example of servant leadership. Cathy built his business on Christian principles, particularly emphasizing servant leadership—putting others' needs first, demonstrating humility, and valuing employees and customers alike. He believed that serving others with humility wasn't just ethical but essential for effective leadership. Cathy made it a point to treat employees like family, emphasizing work-life balance, respect, and a supportive culture. This approach, deeply inspired by his Christian faith, extended to Chick-fil-A's customer service model, which remains renowned for kindness and courtesy. His faith-based leadership was grounded in the principle that by serving and uplifting others, a leader creates a thriving, loyal team and an enduring legacy (Cathy, 2007).

Prayer

"God, help me to be a leader who honors You. Give me the courage to lead by example, the love to influence others positively, and the humility to know when to follow. Help me to encourage my friends and to step out boldly as a leader who shines Your light. Amen."

CONFLICT RESOLUTION

Practical Challenge

Choose one conflict in your life that needs resolution. Pray for God's wisdom and guidance, then take steps to approach the person involved, listen well, and seek a peaceful resolution. Be willing to apologize or forgive as needed.

Day 1: How to Approach Someone When You're Upset

Scripture: *Matthew 18:15* - "'If another believer sins against you, go privately and point out the offense. If the other person listens and confesses it, you have won that person back." (NLT)

Reflection: When conflict arises, it's natural to want to react in anger or avoid the issue altogether. But Jesus teaches us to handle conflict with love and directness. Instead of gossiping or holding a grudge, go directly to the person involved, and speak calmly and honestly about what upset you. This approach shows respect and gives an opportunity for understanding and reconciliation.

Journal Question: How do you usually respond to conflict? How can you approach it in a healthier way?

Day 2: The Importance of Listening During Conflict

Scripture: *James 1:19* - "Understand this, my dear brothers and sisters: You must all be quick to listen, slow to speak, and slow to get angry." (NLT)

Reflection: Listening is key to resolving conflict. It shows that you care about the other person's perspective and are willing to understand their side of the story. Being slow to speak and quick to listen helps reduce misunderstandings and anger. Next time you find yourself in a disagreement, pause and make an effort to listen before responding.

Journal Question: Think about the last couple of times you found yourself in a disagreement. Did you spend more time listening or more time speaking (or thinking about what you wanted to say next)? How can you be a better listener during disagreements?

Day 3: Seeking Peaceful Resolutions Based on Love and Respect

Scripture: *Romans 12:18* - "If it is possible, as far as it depends on you, live at peace with everyone." (NIV)

Reflection: God calls us to be peacemakers, seeking to resolve conflicts in a loving and respectful way. This doesn't mean avoiding difficult conversations, but approaching them with a heart of reconciliation and a desire to make things right. Strive to resolve conflicts in a way that brings peace and shows love, reflecting God's heart for unity and harmony.

Journal Question: What is one conflict in your life that you need to resolve by going directly to the person involved?

Day 4: When to Apologize and Ask for Forgiveness

Scripture: *Matthew 5:23-24* - "'Therefore, if you are offering your gift at the altar and there remember that your brother or sister has something against you, leave your gift there in front of the altar. First go and be reconciled to them; then come and offer your gift." (NIV)

Reflection: Jesus teaches that reconciliation is so important that it should take priority over religious rituals. If you know that someone has something against you, take the first step to apologize and make things right. Asking for forgiveness brings healing to relationships and honors God. Don't let pride keep you from taking the initiative to apologize and seek peace.

Journal Question: Is there someone who you need to ask forgiveness from? What do you need to do to create the space for that to happen?

Day 5: Handling Ongoing Conflict with Grace

Scripture: *Ephesians 4:2-3* - "Always be humble and gentle. Be patient with each other, making allowance for each other's faults because of your love. Make every effort to keep yourselves united in the Spirit, binding yourselves together with peace." (NLT)

Reflection: Not all conflicts are resolved quickly, and some may be ongoing. In these cases, God calls us to respond with humility, gentleness, and patience. Keep showing love, even when it's hard, and do your best to maintain peace. Choose forgiveness as many times as it takes. Trust God to work in the situation and keep praying for wisdom and grace to handle it well.

Journal Question: If you're dealing with ongoing conflict, how can you handle it with more grace, patience, and humility?

Weekly Summary

This week, we explored how to approach conflict with love, a listening ear, and a desire for peace. We learned the importance of apologizing and asking for forgiveness, and how to handle ongoing conflicts with grace. God calls us to be peacemakers, striving for unity and reconciliation in all our relationships.

Real-Life Story

Tony Dungy: Resolving Conflict with Grace Tony Dungy, a former NFL coach and strong Christian leader, often speaks about resolving conflict with grace and patience. He believes that handling conflicts well is essential not just in sports but in all relationships. Dungy encourages forgiveness and understanding, saying, "You have to treat people the way you want to be treated, and that starts with resolving conflict in a loving way."

One notable example where he practiced this comes from his time as head coach of the Indianapolis Colts when he was asked to confront the approach of his former assistant, Lovie Smith, who coached the Chicago Bears. Some fans and media pushed Dungy to create a rivalry narrative leading up to the Super Bowl XLI face-off in 2007, but Dungy resisted. Instead of framing it as a competition against Smith, he showed respect and highlighted their shared values and faith as Christians. Rather than taking an adversarial stance, he publicly expressed admiration for Smith, and they even prayed together before the game.

Dungy's approach diffused tension and fostered mutual respect, helping both coaches feel they could play with dignity rather than hostility. This was significant because it illustrated how Dungy values relationships and personal integrity over public rivalry. His humility and grace in this situation were widely appreciated, setting a powerful example for players and fans alike. His example reminds us that whether we are on a team, in school, or at home, handling conflict with grace and respect reflects God's love (Dungy, 2008).

Prayer

"God, help me to handle conflict with love and grace. Give me the courage to approach others when I'm upset, the patience to listen, and the humility to apologize when I'm wrong. Teach me to be a peacemaker who seeks unity and reflects Your love in all my relationships. Amen."

WEEK 42

FORGIVENESS

Practical Challenge

Identify one person you need to forgive this week. Pray for the strength to forgive them, ask God to help you let go of any bitterness, and take a step toward releasing that person from the debt they owe you. Trust God to bring healing and freedom as you forgive.

Day 1: Understanding What Forgiveness Really Means

Scripture: *Matthew 18:21-22* - "Then Peter came to him and asked, 'Lord, how often should I forgive someone who sins against me? Seven times?'

'No, not seven times,' Jesus replied, 'but seventy times seven!'" (NLT)

Reflection: Forgiveness is a choice to let go of anger, bitterness, and the desire for revenge. It means releasing someone from a debt they owe you, just as God has forgiven you through Jesus. Forgiveness doesn't excuse wrongdoing, but it allows healing to begin. God calls us to forgive because we've been forgiven much, and holding on to anger only harms us.

Journal Question: What does forgiveness mean to you, and why is it important?

Day 2: How Unforgiveness Hurts You More Than Others

Scripture: *Hebrews 12:15* - "Look after each other so that none of you fails to receive the grace of God. Watch out that no poisonous root of bitterness grows up to trouble you, corrupting many." (NLT)

Reflection: Holding onto unforgiveness is like drinking poison and expecting the other person to suffer. It can lead to bitterness that affects not only your heart but your relationships, mental health, and spiritual growth. Letting go of unforgiveness allows you to experience freedom and peace, and it opens the door for God's healing in your life.

Journal Question: Is there someone in your life you need to forgive? How can you begin to take steps toward forgiveness?

Day 3: Offering Forgiveness Even When It's Hard

Scripture: *Matthew 6:14* - "'If you forgive those who sin against you, your heavenly Father will forgive you." (NLT)

Reflection: Forgiving others is almost never easy, especially when the hurt runs deep. But Jesus teaches us that offering forgiveness is essential to living in His grace. When you choose to forgive, you're not saying that what happened was okay; you're just releasing it to God and choosing to move forward. Pray for God to give you the strength to forgive, even when it's hard.

Journal Question: Can you see any areas of your life where unforgiveness has affected your heart, relationships, or spiritual growth?

Day 4: The Connection Between God's Forgiveness and Ours

Scripture: *Colossians 3:13* - "Make allowance for each other's faults, and forgive anyone who offends you. Remember, the Lord forgave you, so you must forgive others." (NLT)

Reflection: The way we forgive others is directly connected to how God forgives us. If we truly understand the depth of God's forgiveness for our personal sins, we will be more willing to forgive those who have wronged us. Take time to remember the grace you've received from God, and let that motivate you to extend grace to others.

Journal Question: Take some time to meditate on God's forgiveness for you and the death that Jesus endured on your behalf. How can you offer forgiveness to others out of that place of recognizing God's extravagant mercy shown to you?

Day 5: Learning to Forgive Yourself

Scripture: *2 Corinthians 5:17* - "Therefore, if anyone is in Christ, the new creation has come: The old has gone, the new is here!" (NIV)

Reflection: Sometimes, the hardest person to forgive is yourself. But God's forgiveness covers all your mistakes and failures. When you repent and receive His grace, you don't have to hold on to guilt and shame. Part of honoring God's authority and lordship is acknowledging that God is the One who gets to decide whether you are worthy of forgiveness or not - not you. He made that decision already when He sent Jesus to take your punishment in your place. Let go of self-condemnation, accept God's forgiveness, and learn to forgive yourself as well. You are loved and free in Christ!

Journal Question: Are there any areas in your life where you need to forgive yourself and let go of guilt or shame?

Weekly Summary

This week, we learned about the true meaning of forgiveness and how unforgiveness can hurt us more than others. We explored offering forgiveness even when it's hard, understanding the connection between God's forgiveness and ours, and learning to forgive ourselves. Forgiveness brings freedom, peace, and a deeper understanding of God's grace.

Real-Life Story

Corrie Ten Boom: The Power of Forgiveness Corrie Ten Boom, a Dutch Christian who helped many Jews escape the Nazis during World War II, was arrested and sent to Ravensbrück concentration camp for her efforts.

After the war, Corrie dedicated her life to sharing her experiences and the message of forgiveness and healing that she had found in her faith. One of the most poignant moments in her life occurred when she encountered one of the guards from Ravensbrück. This guard had been particularly brutal, and Corrie had experienced great suffering at his hands. Years after the war, while speaking at a church in Munich, she was surprised to see the former guard approach her after her talk.

As he came forward, Corrie recognized him instantly, and a wave of emotions rushed over her. He introduced himself and said, "I have done terrible things, but I have come to ask for your forgiveness." He explained that he had since become a Christian and realized the depths of his wrongdoing. In that moment, Corrie felt a deep conflict within her. Her heart was torn between the pain of her past and the message of forgiveness that she had preached. The memories of the suffering and the loss of her family in the concentration camp flooded back to her. However, she knew that forgiveness was essential for her own healing and that of others.

She prayed for strength, and as she looked at the man before her, she extended her hand to him. She later described the act of reaching out as something she felt she couldn't do on her own; it was only through God's grace that she could offer forgiveness. As their hands touched, Corrie felt an overwhelming sense of love and forgiveness wash over her, both for him and for herself. In that powerful moment, she realized that forgiveness is not just a feeling but an act of the will—a choice to let go of the past and embrace the possibility of healing. This encounter reinforced her belief that God's love transcends all, even the deepest wounds caused by human cruelty (Ten Boom, 2006).

Corrie Ten Boom's story illustrates the incredible power of forgiveness, even in the face of unimaginable suffering, and her life continues to inspire many to seek reconciliation and healing in their own lives. She later said, "Forgiveness is the key that unlocks the door of resentment and the handcuffs of hatred. It is a power that breaks the chains of bitterness and the shackles of selfishness" (Ten Boom, 1982). Corrie's life teaches us that forgiveness, even in the face of deep hurt, is possible through God's grace.

Prayer

"Dear God, thank You for forgiving me of all my sins. Help me to forgive others as You have forgiven me. Take away any bitterness or anger I may be holding onto, and teach me to live in the freedom of forgiveness. Help me to forgive myself and walk in Your grace. Amen."

WEEK 43

SERVING OTHERS

Practical Challenge

Choose one person or place to serve this week. Whether it's a family member, friend, neighbor, or community organization, look for an opportunity to serve without expecting anything in return. Ask God to use your service to show His love to others.

Day 1: Why Serving Others is Part of Following Jesus

Scripture: *Philippians 2:5-8* - "In your relationships with one another, have the same mindset as Christ Jesus: Who, being in very nature God, did not consider equality with God something to be used to his own advantage; rather, he made himself nothing by taking the very nature of a servant, being made in human likeness. And being found in appearance as a man, he humbled himself by becoming obedient to death— even death on a cross!" (NIV)

Reflection: Jesus is our ultimate example of serving others. He didn't come to be served, even though He is the only one who truly deserves all service and honor. Rather, he came to serve those around Him, even to the point of giving His life. Following Jesus means living a life of service, putting the needs of others before our own. When we serve others, we reflect the love and humility of Christ.

Journal Question: How does Jesus' example of service inspire you to serve others more?

Day 2: Small Ways to Serve Those Around You Daily

Scripture: *Galatians 5:13* - "For you have been called to live in freedom, my brothers and sisters. But don't use your freedom to satisfy your sinful nature. Instead, use your freedom to serve one another in love." (NLT)

Reflection: Serving others doesn't always have to be something big or grand; it can be as simple as helping a friend with homework, listening to someone who's struggling, or offering encouragement to a classmate. Small acts of service, done with love, can make a huge difference. Look for little ways to serve those around you every day.

Journal Question: What are some small ways you can serve those around you daily?

Day 3: Serving with a Humble Heart, Without Expecting Anything in Return

Scripture: *Acts 20:35* - "And I have been a constant example of how you can help those in need by working hard. You should remember the words of the Lord Jesus: 'It is more blessed to give than to receive.'" (NLT)

Reflection: True service comes from a humble heart — one that serves without seeking recognition, praise, or anything in return. Jesus served others selflessly, and He calls us to do the same. When you serve out of love and humility, without expecting anything back, you reflect God's heart and experience the joy that comes from putting others first.

Journal Question: Why is it important to serve with a humble heart, without expecting anything in return?

Day 4: How Service Helps You Grow Closer to God

Scripture: *Matthew 25:40* - "'The King will reply, "Truly I tell you, whatever you did for one of the least of these brothers and sisters of mine, you did for me."'" (NIV)

Reflection: Serving others is one of the ways we grow closer to God. When we serve "the least of these" — those who are hurting, lonely, or in need — we are serving Jesus Himself. Acts of service draw us closer to God's heart and deepen our relationship with Him. Each time you serve, know that God sees and is pleased.

Journal Question: How has serving others helped you grow closer to God in the past?

Day 5: The Impact of Serving in Your Community

Scripture: *Romans 12:6-8* - "We have different gifts, according to the grace given to each of us. If your gift is prophesying, then prophesy in accordance with your faith; if it is serving, then serve; if it is teaching, then teach; if it is to encourage, then give encouragement; if it is giving, then give generously; if it is to lead, do it diligently; if it is to show mercy, do it cheerfully." (NIV)

Reflection: Serving in your community is a powerful way to use the gifts God has given you. Your time, your resources, and your talents are all gifts from God that he has given you to steward with generosity. Whether through volunteering at church, helping a neighbor, or reaching out to those in need, your service can have a lasting impact on those around you. You are God's hands and feet in your community, and your willingness to serve can be a powerful testimony of God's love.

Journal Question: What are some of your unique talents, spiritual gifts, or resources that you can use to serve your community this week to make an impact for God?

Weekly Summary

This week, we focused on the importance of serving others as part of following Jesus. We learned how small acts of service can make a big difference, how to serve with humility, and how serving others helps us grow closer to God. Serving in your community is a way to use your gifts for God's glory and impact those around you with His love.

Real-Life Story

Mother Teresa: A Life of Selfless Service Mother Teresa dedicated her life to serving the poorest of the poor in India. One powerful story of Mother Teresa's compassion involves a man she found lying in a Calcutta gutter, extremely ill and covered in sores. Many people had walked by him, dismissing him as just another beggar, but she saw his suffering and decided to care for him herself. She took him to her home for the dying, where she washed and cleaned his wounds, fed him, and stayed by his side. Despite his pain, he felt love and dignity for the first time in years. In his final moments, he told her, "I have lived like an animal in the streets, but I am going to die like an angel, loved and cared for" (Nobel Prize Outreach AB 2024, Nov. 2024)

This small but profound act reflects how Mother Teresa saw every person as worthy of love and care. Her unwavering commitment to showing kindness to individuals, one at a time, defined her approach to service. Her selfless acts of love and service touched countless lives and inspired others to serve. Mother Teresa's life reminds us that serving others doesn't have to be complicated — it's about showing love in practical ways and putting others before ourselves.

Prayer

"Dear God, thank You for the example of Jesus, who came to serve others with humility and love. Help me to see opportunities to serve those around me each day. Give me a humble heart that seeks to serve without expecting anything in return, and use my service to draw others closer to You. Amen."

LOVING PEOPLE WHO ARE HARD TO LOVE

Practical Challenge

Choose one person who has been difficult for you to love and begin praying for them daily. Ask God to soften your heart, help you forgive, and show you practical ways to love them with God's love. Look for opportunities to show kindness to them throughout the week.

Day 1: God's Command to Love Your Enemies

Scripture: *Matthew 5:44* - "But I say to you, love your enemies, bless those who curse you, do good to those who hate you, and pray for those who spitefully use you and persecute you," (NKJV)

Reflection: It's easy to love people who love you back, but Jesus calls us to go further — to love even our enemies and those who hurt us. Loving difficult people is not a suggestion; it's a command. When we choose to love our enemies, we reflect the unconditional love of God and allow His light to shine through us in powerful ways.

Journal Question: Who is someone in your life that you find difficult to love, and how can you start showing them love?

Day 2: Practical Ways to Show Love to Difficult People

Scripture: *Romans 12:20* - "Instead, 'If your enemies are hungry, feed them. If they are thirsty, give them something to drink. In doing this, you will heap burning coals of shame on their heads.'" (NLT)

Reflection: Loving difficult people requires action. It means showing kindness when you feel like retaliating, serving when you feel like ignoring, and praying for those who mistreat you. Look for practical ways to love those who are hard to love — maybe by offering a kind word, doing something thoughtful for them, or simply choosing to forgive.

Journal Question: What are some practical ways you can show kindness to someone who has hurt or mistreated you?

Day 3: Setting Boundaries While Still Loving Others

Scripture: *2 Timothy 3:2-5* - "For people will love only themselves and their money. They will be boastful and proud, scoffing at God, disobedient to their parents, and ungrateful. They will consider nothing sacred. They will be unloving and unforgiving; they will slander others and have no self-control. They will be cruel and hate what is good. They will betray their friends, be reckless, be puffed up with pride, and love pleasure rather than God. They will act religious, but they will reject the power that could make them godly. Stay away from people like that!" (NLT)

Reflection: Loving people doesn't mean allowing them to walk all over you. It's important to recognize when someone in your life is not healthy or safe to be around and set healthy boundaries to protect your heart and well-being. Loving others is about showing grace and kindness, but it's also about knowing when to step back and create space. Boundaries help you love from a place of strength and not become overwhelmed by toxic behavior. Seek God's wisdom in this area through His Word and by His Spirit that leads you in agreement with His Word.

Journal Question: How can setting healthy boundaries help you love others in a balanced way?

Day 4: Praying for Those Who Hurt or Mistreat You

Scripture: *Luke 6:28* - "bless those who curse you, pray for those who mistreat you." (NIV)

Reflection: One of the most powerful ways to love someone who's hard to love is by praying for them. When you pray for those who have hurt you, you invite God to work in their hearts and in yours. Praying for your enemies helps you let go of bitterness, see them through God's eyes, and trust God to bring healing and change.

Journal Question: Who do you need to start praying for regularly as an act of forgiveness and love?

Day 5: How Loving Difficult People Changes Your Heart

Scripture: *1 John 4:7* - "Beloved, let us love one another, for love is of God; and everyone who loves is born of God and knows God." (NKJV)

Reflection: Loving and praying for difficult people isn't just about changing them — it's about changing your own heart. As you learn to love those who are hard to love, God works in your heart, growing compassion, patience, and grace. This kind of love is a reflection of God's love for us, and it helps us grow to be more like Him.

Journal Question: How has loving difficult people changed your heart and helped you grow closer to God?

Weekly Summary

This week, we learned about loving people who are hard to love, as God commands us to love our enemies. We explored practical ways to show love, the importance of setting boundaries, praying for those who hurt us, and how loving others changes our hearts. Loving difficult people is not easy, but it brings us closer to God and allows His love to shine through us.

Real-Life Story

Dr. Martin Luther King Jr.: Loving Your Enemies Dr. Martin Luther King Jr. led a movement of non-violence and love in the face of racism and hatred. He preached about loving your enemies and famously said, "Love is the only force capable of transforming an enemy into a friend" (King, 2012). One of the most famous examples of Martin Luther King Jr. showing love to an "enemy" happened in 1960, during a book signing in Harlem. A woman named Izola Curry approached him, asked if he was really Martin Luther King Jr., and when he confirmed, she plunged a letter opener into his chest. The blade was lodged dangerously close to his aorta, and doctors said any sudden movement could have killed him.

King underwent surgery and survived. Despite the attack, he publicly expressed no anger toward Curry. Instead, he later reflected on the incident, showing compassion and empathy for her troubled state of mind. He acknowledged the difficulties faced by those who harbor such hatred and spoke of his desire for people to respond with understanding and love, even in the face of violence. King's response showed his deep commitment to nonviolence and the transformative power of love and forgiveness, even toward someone who had intended to take his life. Despite facing persecution, he chose to respond with love and grace, showing the power of God's love to change hearts and bring about peace. Dr. King's life teaches us that loving difficult people is not just about being nice — it's a powerful way to bring God's love and transformation to the world (*Curry, Izola Ware*, The Martin Luther King, Jr. Research and Education Institute).

Prayer

"God, thank You for loving me even when I was difficult to love. Help me to love others in the same way, even when it's hard. Teach me to pray for those who hurt me, set healthy boundaries, and show kindness to all people. Change my heart to reflect Your love in everything I do. Amen."

WEEK 45

BEING KIND IN A HARSH WORLD

Practical Challenge

Look for one opportunity each day this week to show kindness to someone, especially those who may not expect it. Whether it's through encouraging words, helping someone with a need, paying it forward, or simply being a good listener, choose to reflect God's love through your actions.

Day 1: Why Kindness Matters More Than Ever

Scripture: *Ephesians 4:32* - "And be kind to one another, tenderhearted, forgiving one another, even as God in Christ forgave you." (NKJV)

Reflection: Kindness is a powerful way to reflect God's love in a world that can be harsh and unkind. Even simple acts of kindness can have a profound impact on those around you, showing them the compassion and grace that God has shown you. Every day you have an opportunity to choose kindness and be a light to those who may be struggling or hurting.

Journal Question: When was the last time someone's kindness made a difference in your day? How did it make you feel?

Day 2: The Ripple Effect of Small Acts of Kindness

Scripture: *Proverbs 16:24* - "Pleasant words *are like* a honeycomb, sweetness to the soul and health to the bones." (NKJV)

Reflection: One small act of kindness can make a huge difference in someone's day. A kind word, a smile, or helping someone in need can bring healing, encouragement, and hope. Your actions don't have to be big to be meaningful — sometimes the smallest gestures have the greatest impact. Each act of kindness creates a ripple effect, inspiring others to do the same.

Journal Question: What are some small acts of kindness you can do to encourage those around you?

Day 3: Overcoming the Temptation to Be Harsh or Cruel

Scripture: *Colossians 3:12* - "Therefore, as God's chosen people, holy and dearly loved, clothe yourselves with compassion, kindness, humility, gentleness and patience." (NIV)

Reflection: It's easy to be harsh, especially when others are rude or difficult. But God calls you to be different — to clothe yourself with kindness, compassion, and gentleness, even when it's hard. Overcoming the temptation to respond with anger or cruelty means choosing to show love, even when others don't deserve it. Remember, God has shown you great kindness, and He wants you to show that same kindness to others.

Journal Question: How can you overcome the temptation to respond with harshness when you're treated poorly?

Day 4: How to Respond with Kindness in Tough Situations

Scripture: *Luke 6:31* - "Do to others as you would like them to do to you." (NLT)

Reflection: Responding with kindness in tough situations is not always easy, but it's what God desires. When others treat you poorly, respond the way you would want to be treated — with patience, understanding, and love. This doesn't mean allowing others to mistreat you, but choosing to reflect Christ's love in your response, even when it's hard.

Journal Question: How does God respond to you when you make mistakes? How do you wish other people responded to you when you make a poor decision? How can you respond to others with kindness in a way that reflects how you hope to be treated?

Day 5: Kindness as a Reflection of God's Love

Scripture: *Titus 3:4-5* - "But when the kindness and love of God our Savior appeared, he saved us, not because of righteous things we had done, but because of his mercy. He saved us through the washing of rebirth and renewal by the Holy Spirit," (NIV)

Reflection: God's kindness led to our salvation, and He calls us to reflect that kindness to others. When you show kindness, you reflect the heart of God and make His love known to the world. Choose to be an instrument of God's kindness, showing love, mercy, and compassion to everyone you meet.

Journal Question: In what areas of your life can you show more kindness and compassion, even to those who may not deserve it?

Weekly Summary

This week, we learned about the importance of kindness in a harsh world and how small acts of kindness can make a big difference. We discussed overcoming the temptation to be harsh, responding with kindness in difficult situations, and how kindness is a reflection of God's love. By choosing kindness, you can be a light in a dark world and point others to Jesus.

Real-Life Story

Fred Rogers (Mr. Rogers): Spreading Kindness One Person at a Time Fred Rogers, known as "Mr. Rogers," was the beloved host of *Mister Rogers' Neighborhood*, a children's television program that focused on kindness, love, and understanding. Fred was known for saying, "There are three ways to ultimate success: The first way is to be kind. The second way is to be kind. The third way is to be kind" (Harris, 2013). Fred Rogers demonstrated his commitment to kindness and compassion in countless ways off-screen. One touching example involved a young boy with cerebral palsy who was a longtime fan of *Mister Rogers' Neighborhood*. The boy's condition made it challenging for him to express his emotions, but his family arranged for him to meet Fred Rogers in person. When Rogers arrived, the boy became so overwhelmed that he started hitting himself out of frustration. Rather than showing discomfort or backing away, Rogers immediately knelt beside the boy, took his hand gently, and began speaking softly to him. Then he asked the boy, "Would you do something for me? Would you pray for me?" The boy was stunned, as he felt he had nothing to offer someone like Fred Rogers, but the request empowered him. Later, Rogers explained to those around him that asking for help can be one of the greatest ways to show love and respect for someone else (Brooks, 2018).

Rogers's sensitivity and his request for the boy's prayers transformed what could have been an awkward encounter into a moment of deep connection, kindness, and dignity. Mr. Rogers demonstrated that small acts of kindness could make a lasting impact on both children and adults alike. His life encourages us to spread kindness, one person at a time, and to live out God's love in our daily interactions.

Prayer

"God, thank You for Your kindness toward me. Help me to be kind to others, even in difficult situations, and to spread Your love through my words and actions. Let my kindness be a reflection of who You are and a light in a harsh world. Amen."

Building Bridges, Not Walls

Practical Challenge

Choose one person you don't know very well or someone who is different from you and make an effort to connect with them this week. Look for common ground, listen to their story, and be intentional about building a bridge of understanding and friendship.

Day 1: The Importance of Empathy and Understanding

Scripture: *Romans 12:15* - "Rejoice with those who rejoice, and weep with those who weep." (NKJV)

Reflection: Building bridges begins with empathy — being willing to understand and share the feelings of others. Empathy allows you to connect with people on a deeper level, to celebrate with them in good times, and to comfort them in their struggles. When you take the time to see things from another person's perspective, you begin to break down walls and build meaningful connections.

Journal Question: How can you practice empathy and understanding in your relationships this week?

Day 2: How to Find Common Ground with People Different from You

Scripture: *1 Corinthians 9:22* - "When I am with those who are weak, I share their weakness, for I want to bring the weak to Christ. Yes, I try to find common ground with everyone, doing everything I can to save some." (NLT)

Reflection: Finding common ground with those who are different from you is a powerful way to build bridges. Whether it's through shared interests, values, struggles, or experiences, focusing on what you have in common helps you connect and build understanding. Paul became "all things to all people" to share the love of Christ — you, too, can build bridges by being willing to relate to others on their level.

Journal Question: What are some ways you can find common ground with people who are different from you in your community, school, or neighborhood?

Day 3: Overcoming Prejudice and Stereotypes

Scripture: *James 2:1* - "My dear brothers and sisters, how can you claim to have faith in our glorious Lord Jesus Christ if you favor some people over others?" (NLT)

Reflection: Prejudice and stereotypes create walls that divide us. God calls you to see people as He sees them — not through the lens of bias, but with love and acceptance. Overcoming prejudice means choosing to treat everyone with kindness, respect, and equality, regardless of their background or differences. By doing so, you break down walls and build bridges of understanding and love.

Journal Question: Are there any prejudices or stereotypes you need to overcome to build better connections with others?

Day 4: Building Meaningful Connections with Others

Scripture: *Psalm 133:1&3* - "How wonderful and pleasant it is when brothers live together in harmony! Harmony is as refreshing as the dew from Mount

Hermon that falls on the mountains of Zion. And there the Lord has pronounced his blessing, even life everlasting." (NLT)

Reflection: Building meaningful connections requires effort and intentionality. It means reaching out to others, spending time together, and encouraging one another in love. As you make the effort to connect with others, you not only build bridges but also create a supportive and loving community where people can grow in faith and life together.

Journal Question: How can you be intentional about building meaningful connections and encouraging others in love in your communities and spheres of influence?

Day 5: The Power of Unity in Christ Despite Differences

Scripture: *Galatians 3:28* - "There is neither Jew nor Gentile, neither slave nor free, nor is there male and female, for you are all one in Christ Jesus." (NIV)

Reflection: In Christ, we are all united as one body. Despite our differences — race, culture, background, or status — we are called to live in unity. This unity in Christ breaks down the walls that divide us and allows us to build bridges of love, acceptance, and understanding. Let God's love be the bridge that unites us, and let's celebrate our differences as part of God's beautiful creation.

Journal Question: How does embracing unity in Christ help you to see people through God's eyes and build bridges across differences?

Weekly Summary

This week, we explored the importance of building bridges instead of walls. We discussed empathy, finding common ground, overcoming prejudice, building meaningful connections, and the power of unity in Christ. Building bridges allows us to connect with others, break down barriers, and reflect God's love in our relationships.

Real-Life Story

William and Catherine Booth: Building Bridges to the Poor William and Catherine Booth, founders of The Salvation Army, dedicated their lives to building bridges to those who were often ignored — the poor, the addicted, and the homeless. They believed that every person deserved to hear the gospel and be treated with dignity and respect. One powerful story of William and Catherine Booth overcoming prejudice to serve others occurred in the early days of their ministry in London's East End. At the time, the area was riddled with poverty, alcoholism, and crime, and the destitute people living there were often looked down upon by society, even by many churches. One evening, William Booth encountered a man who was lying unconscious in a gutter, drunk and visibly neglected. Many others walked past, dismissing him as a hopeless "drunkard" unworthy of help. However, Booth saw the man's suffering rather than his reputation. He knelt beside him, helped him up, and personally escorted him to a nearby shelter, where he made sure the man was fed, given new clothes, and provided with a place to sleep.

This was no isolated act; Booth and his wife, Catherine, were known for rejecting societal stereotypes and welcoming people society shunned, treating them with dignity and compassion. Their unwavering commitment to seeing value in everyone became a foundational principle of The Salvation Army, which they founded as a movement to break down barriers and bring hope to the marginalized and outcast. By meeting both physical and spiritual needs, the Booths broke down walls of prejudice and showed the love of Christ to those who were hurting (Green, 2006).

Prayer

"God, help me to build bridges of love and understanding with those around me. Teach me to show empathy, overcome prejudice, and find unity in Christ with all people. Let my life be a reflection of Your love that breaks down walls and brings people together. Amen."

WEEK 47

DEALING WITH GOSSIP AND BULLYING

Practical Challenge

If you notice gossip or bullying happening around you this week, choose to walk away from the gossip or speak up to defend the person being hurt. Be a voice for encouragement and protection, and let God's love shine through your words and actions.

Day 1: The Damaging Effects of Gossip on Relationships

Scripture: *Proverbs 16:28* - "A troublemaker plants seeds of strife; gossip separates the best of friends." (NLT)

Reflection: Gossip can tear apart friendships, cause misunderstandings, and damage trust. Talking about others behind their backs might seem harmless, but it nearly always leads to hurt and division. God calls us to use our words to build others up, not to tear them down. Before speaking about someone else, consider whether your words will bring life or harm.

Journal Question: How have you seen gossip affect your friendships or relationships?

Day 2: How to Avoid Participating in Gossip

Scripture: *Ephesians 4:29* - "Don't use foul or abusive language. Let everything you say be good and helpful, so that your words will be an encouragement to those who hear them." (NLT)

Reflection: It can be tempting to join in when others start gossiping, but God calls us to be different. Avoiding gossip means choosing to speak words that are kind, helpful, and uplifting. When you hear others gossiping, change the subject or walk away. Remember, your words have power — use them to encourage and bring life.

Journal Question: What steps can you take to avoid participating in gossip and to use your words to encourage others instead?

Day 3: What to Do if You're the Victim of Bullying

Scripture: *Psalm 34:17* - *"The righteous* cry out, and the Lord hears, and delivers them out of all their troubles." (NKJV)

Reflection: If you are being bullied, know that you are not alone. God sees your pain and is with you in your struggles. Don't be afraid to reach out to a trusted friend, adult, or counselor for help and support. Remember that your worth and identity come from God, and no one has the right to tear you down or make you feel less than who you are.

Journal Question: If you have been bullied, how can you remind yourself of God's love and seek support from trusted people?

Day 4: Standing Up for Others Who Are Being Bullied

Scripture: *Proverbs 31:8-9* - "Speak up for those who cannot speak for themselves; ensure justice for those being crushed. Yes, speak up for the poor and helpless, and see that they get justice." (NLT)

Reflection: God calls you to be an advocate for those who are mistreated. If you see someone being bullied, don't stay silent. Stand up for them, offer support, and let them know they're not alone. Enlist help from trusted adults on their behalf if needed. Speaking up for others is a powerful way to show God's love. Be the voice that defends and protects those who are vulnerable.

Journal Question: Who do you know who is bullied or mistreated often? How can you stand up for them?

Day 5: Seeking Help When Bullying Becomes Dangerous

Scripture: *Psalm 82:3-4* - "Defend the weak and the fatherless; uphold the cause of the poor and the oppressed. Rescue the weak and the needy; deliver them from the hand of the wicked." (NIV)

Reflection: If bullying becomes physical, dangerous, or makes you feel unsafe, it's important to seek help immediately. Find a trusted adult, school counselor, or teacher who can intervene and provide support. God does not want you to suffer alone, and seeking help is a way to protect yourself and others from harm.

Journal Question: Who can you turn to for help if you or someone else is facing dangerous bullying?

Weekly Summary

This week, we explored how gossip and bullying can damage relationships and how we are called to be different. We learned how to avoid gossip, stand up against bullying, and seek help when needed. God calls us to use our words to build others up, defend the weak, and show His love through our actions.

Real-Life Story

Nick Vujicic: Overcoming Bullying with Courage Nick Vujicic, born without arms and legs due to a rare condition called tetra-amelia syndrome, faced significant challenges from a young age, including bullying. Growing up in Australia, he often felt isolated and different from his peers, which made him a target for taunts and ridicule at school. The hurtful comments and bullying made him feel like he didn't belong and led him to experience deep feelings of loneliness and despair. Despite the hardships he faced, Nick's faith played a crucial role in helping him navigate these difficult times. His parents instilled in him a strong Christian foundation, teaching him the value of inner strength and the importance of trusting God's plan for his life. In moments of bullying, he would often turn to prayer, seeking comfort and strength from his relationship with God.

One pivotal moment came during his teenage years when the bullying reached a peak. Nick was invited to speak at his school about his life and experiences. Although he was initially apprehensive about sharing his story, he decided to embrace the opportunity, believing it could help others understand his journey and perhaps foster empathy among his peers. As he stood before his classmates, Nick spoke openly about his struggles, his faith, and the importance of kindness. He shared how he found hope and purpose in God despite the challenges he faced. His vulnerability resonated with many students, and rather than condemnation, he received support and understanding from those who had once bullied him.

This experience not only helped to change the narrative around his life at school but also ignited a passion within Nick to advocate for others facing similar challenges. He realized that his story could inspire many people around the world. From that point on, he began speaking publicly about his faith and experiences, using his platform to encourage others to rise above adversity. Nick Vujicic's journey is a testament to the strength that can come from faith, resilience, and the power of vulnerability. Instead of allowing bullying to define him, he turned his pain into purpose, helping countless others find hope and strength in their own struggles. He says, "If you can't get a miracle, become one" (Vujicic, 2010). His message of love, acceptance, and faith continues to inspire people of all ages, proving that even in the face of hardship, we can rise and make a difference in the lives of others.

Prayer

"Lord, help me to use my words to build others up and to avoid gossip that can damage relationships. Give me courage to stand up against bullying and to support those who are being mistreated. Let me be a voice of love, encouragement, and protection, reflecting Your heart to those around me. Amen."

HONESTY IN RELATIONSHIPS

Practical Challenge

Identify one area of your life where you need to be more honest, whether it's with a friend, family member, or even yourself. Take steps this week to speak the truth in love, ask for forgiveness if needed, and commit to living with integrity in that area.

Day 1: The Foundation of Trust in Any Relationship

Scripture: *Proverbs 12:22* - "The Lord detests lying lips, but he delights in people who are trustworthy." (NIV)

Reflection: Trust is the foundation of any healthy relationship, and honesty is key to building that trust. When you choose to be truthful, others see that they can rely on you and believe what you say. Honesty is more than just not lying — it's being open, genuine, and reliable in all you do. Choose to be a person of integrity, and let your relationships be built on trust.

Journal Question: How has honesty played a role in building trust in your relationships?

Day 2: How to Be Honest Without Being Hurtful

Scripture: *Ephesians 4:15* - "Instead, speaking the truth in love, we will grow to become in every respect the mature body of him who is the head, that is, Christ." (NIV)

Reflection: Being honest doesn't mean saying whatever comes to mind without considering how it may affect others. God calls us to speak the truth in love — to be honest while being kind, compassionate, and considerate. Before speaking, think about how you can share your thoughts in a way that builds others up and encourages growth. Honesty should never be used as an excuse to hurt others but rather as a way to foster deeper connections based on love and understanding.

Journal Question: What are some ways you can speak the truth in love, even when it's difficult?

Day 3: The Consequences of Lying or Deceit

Scripture: *Proverbs 19:9* - "A false witness will not go unpunished, and a liar will be destroyed." (NLT)

Reflection: Lying and deceit have serious consequences — they damage relationships, create mistrust, and lead to further sin. Lies can break down the foundation of trust and cause harm to yourself and others. Even small lies can have big impacts. God desires for you to live in truth and integrity, avoiding the path of deceit. Choose honesty, even when it's difficult.

Journal Question: Have you ever experienced the consequences of dishonesty in your life or relationships? How did it affect you?

Day 4: How to Rebuild Trust After It's Broken

Scripture: *James 5:16* - "Confess your sins to each other and pray for each other so that you may be healed. The earnest prayer of a righteous person has great power and produces wonderful results." (NLT)

Reflection: If you've broken someone's trust through dishonesty, rebuilding that trust takes time, humility, and genuine effort. Confessing and asking for forgiveness is the first step to making things right. Be patient and consistent in your actions to show that you are trustworthy. With God's help, relationships can be healed and trust can be restored.

Journal Question: If you've broken someone's trust, how can you begin to rebuild that relationship through honesty and asking forgiveness?

Day 5: Valuing Honesty in Your Friendships and Family

Scripture: *Colossians 3:9-10* - Don't lie to each other, for you have stripped off your old sinful nature and all its wicked deeds. Put on your new nature, and be renewed as you learn to know your Creator and become like him." (NLT)

Reflection: As a follower of Jesus, you are called to live in truth, leaving behind dishonesty and deceit. Valuing honesty in your friendships and family relationships honors God and reflects His character. Make honesty a core value in your life, striving to be truthful in all you say and do. When you live in truth, you honor God and build strong, healthy relationships.

Journal Question: How can you make honesty a core value in your friendships and family relationships?

Weekly Summary

This week, we focused on the importance of honesty as the foundation of trust in any relationship. We learned how to speak the truth in love, the consequences of lying, how to rebuild trust after it's broken, and how to value honesty in all areas of life. Honesty reflects God's character and helps you build genuine, trustworthy connections with others.

Real-Life Story

Abraham Lincoln: Honesty and Integrity Abraham Lincoln's dedication to honesty is famously illustrated by an incident early in his career. In a case involving a man who was overcharged by a storekeeper, Lincoln discovered that his client had already been paid a significant amount, which meant he was attempting to extort more money. Despite the potential to earn a larger fee, Lincoln chose to tell the truth and advised his client to settle fairly. His honesty earned him the nickname "Honest Abe" and cemented his reputation as a lawyer of integrity. He believed that character and integrity were paramount. Lincoln's adherence to honesty, even when it did not benefit him directly, laid the groundwork for his legacy as one of America's most respected leaders. His example of integrity in the face of adversity continues to inspire many to value honesty and ethical behavior in all aspects of life, demonstrating that true character is often revealed in the choices we make when faced with difficult situations (Carwardine, 2007).

Prayer

"God, thank You for being a God of truth. Help me to be honest in all my words and actions, and to speak the truth in love. When I struggle with honesty, remind me of Your call to live with integrity and build trust. Let my relationships be built on the foundation of truth so that I may honor You. Amen."

WEEK 49

HOW TO ENCOURAGE OTHERS

Practical Challenge

Choose one person each day this week to encourage. Whether through words, actions, or prayers, find ways to uplift those around you. Let your encouragement reflect God's love and bring joy to others.

Day 1: The Power of Words to Lift People Up

Scripture: *Proverbs 18:21* - "The tongue can bring death or life; those who love to talk will reap the consequences." (NLT)

Reflection: Your words carry great power — the power to build up or tear down, to encourage or discourage. When you speak words of life, you bring hope, comfort, and strength to those who hear them. Think about the words you use daily — are they uplifting and kind? Use your words to encourage others and speak life into their situations.

Journal Question: How have words of encouragement impacted your life? How can you use your words to uplift others?

Day 2: Recognizing When Someone Needs Encouragement

Scripture: *1 Thessalonians 5:14* - "And we urge you, brothers and sisters, warn those who are idle and disruptive, encourage the disheartened, help the weak, be patient with everyone." (NIV)

Reflection: Not everyone openly asks for encouragement, but it's often needed more than you know. Look for signs that someone might be struggling — a friend who seems down, a classmate who is stressed, or a family member who is more quiet than usual. Taking time to notice others' needs and offering a kind word, a note, or a prayer can make a big difference in their day.

Journal Question: Who in your life seems to be struggling and in need of encouragement? How can you encourage them today?

Day 3: Small Ways to Encourage Others Daily

Scripture: *Matthew 10:42* - "And if you give even a cup of cold water to one of the least of my followers, you will surely be rewarded." (NLT)

Reflection: Encouragement doesn't have to be something big — it can be found in small, everyday actions. A smile, a compliment, a text message, or a word of thanks can brighten someone's day and remind them they are loved and valued. Think of ways you can make encouragement a daily habit, spreading God's love and joy through simple acts.

Journal Question: What are some small ways you can make encouragement a daily habit?

Day 4: Encouragement as a Reflection of God's Love

Scripture: *Romans 15:5* - "May God, who gives this patience and encouragement, help you live in complete harmony with each other, as is fitting for followers of Christ Jesus." (NLT)

Reflection: God is the ultimate source of encouragement, and when you encourage others, you reflect His love. Encouragement helps build faith, renews hope, and draws people closer to God. When you choose to uplift others, you become a vessel of God's love, spreading His light in a world that needs it.

Journal Question: How does encouraging others reflect God's love, and how can it bring them closer to Him?

Day 5: Being a Source of Positivity in Tough Times

Scripture: *Psalm 106:1-2* - "Praise the Lord! Give thanks to the Lord, for he is good! His faithful love endures forever. Who can list the glorious miracles of the Lord? Who can ever praise him enough?" (NLT)

Reflection: It's easy to focus on the negative, especially in tough times, but God calls you to be a source of positivity. Encourage others to see the good, focus on God's promises, and find hope in the midst of struggles. God is always at work in our lives for our good; we just have to trust Him. Your words of encouragement can bring light to dark situations and remind people of God's presence and love.

Journal Question: How can you be a source of positivity and hope, pointing people toward God's goodness and power, even in difficult times?

Weekly Summary

This week, we focused on the power of encouragement — through your words, noticing others' needs, and daily acts of kindness. Encouraging others is a reflection of God's love, bringing hope, joy, and positivity to those around you. Make it a goal to uplift and encourage everyone you meet, being a source of light and support in their lives.

Real-Life Story

Henri Nouwen: The Son of Encouragement Henri Nouwen, a renowned spiritual writer and priest, greatly influenced Nathan Ball, a young man grappling with his direction in life. Nouwen first met Ball when the latter was volunteering at L'Arche, the community where Nouwen served individuals with intellectual disabilities. From their initial meetings, Nouwen recognized in Ball a deep compassion for others and a strong sense of justice. During their conversations, Nouwen urged Ball to examine the dreams and desires he held close but had yet to fully articulate. With gentle but pointed questions, Nouwen encouraged Ball to consider what he felt called to do beyond societal expectations, emphasizing the importance of pursuing one's life calling, especially when it leads to serving others.

As Ball's mentor, Nouwen took a personal interest in his journey, often writing letters filled with encouragement and wisdom. In one of these letters, Nouwen told Ball to listen closely to his own heart and to be unafraid of taking the less conventional path if that was where he felt most alive and useful. Nouwen believed that God called people not just to succeed but to find meaning in service, and he saw in Ball a unique potential to do transformative work. This mentorship gave Ball a new perspective on his aspirations; Nouwen's guidance became a spiritual foundation that Ball returned to time and again as he weighed his options.

Ball ultimately decided to pursue his calling with renewed focus, eventually dedicating his life to working in community-centered missions. He credited Nouwen's mentorship as one of the pivotal influences that helped him define and commit to his path. Nouwen's encouragement to follow his dreams became a guiding principle, urging Ball to not only embrace his own gifts but also to support others in discovering theirs. This mentorship left a lasting legacy in Ball's life, illustrating how faith-driven encouragement can inspire someone to move boldly toward their life's purpose (O'Laughlin, 2009).

Prayer

"Lord, thank You for the power of encouragement. Help me to use my words to build others up, to recognize when someone needs encouragement, and to be a source of positivity and hope. Let my encouragement reflect Your love and bring joy to those around me. Amen."

BEING A GOOD BROTHER

(If you're an only child, use this week to focus on your relationships with brothers and sisters in Christ.)

Practical Challenge

Choose one specific way to show love and support to your sibling(s) this week. Whether it's spending time together, helping them with a need, or praying for them, make an intentional effort to be a good brother or sister and reflect God's love in your family.

Day 1: What It Means to Be a Good Sibling

Scripture: *Proverbs 17:17* - "A friend is always loyal, and a brother is born to help in time of need." (NLT)

Reflection: Siblings are a special gift from God, designed to walk through life together and support each other in all situations. Being a good brother means loving at all times — through joys and struggles. Even when you face challenges or disagreements, remember that God has placed you in each other's lives to be a source of love, support, and encouragement.

Journal Question: How can you strengthen your relationship with your siblings and grow closer as a family?

Day 2: Showing Love and Support to Your Brothers and Sisters

Scripture: *1 John 3:18* - "Dear children, let's not merely say that we love each other; let us show the truth by our actions." (NLT)

Reflection: Love isn't just about saying the right words; it's about showing your love through actions. Supporting your siblings can be as simple as spending time together, helping them with a problem, praying for them, or just being there to listen. Look for ways to show your siblings love in practical ways and be a source of encouragement in their lives.

Journal Question: What are some ways you can show love and support to your siblings this week?

Day 3: Handling Sibling Rivalry with Grace

Scripture: *James 1:19-20* - "My dear brothers and sisters, take note of this: Everyone should be quick to listen, slow to speak and slow to become angry, because human anger does not produce the righteousness that God desires." (NIV)

Reflection: Sibling rivalry is common, but it doesn't have to create lasting tension. When conflicts arise, choose to handle them with grace, humility, and patience. Don't let small disagreements grow into big issues; instead, look for ways to make peace, understand each other's perspectives, and show love even in the midst of arguments.

Journal Question: Think of a recent conflict with a sibling. How did you handle it? How could you have handled it better? How can you handle conflicts and rivalries with grace and patience?

Day 4: Encouraging Your Siblings in Their Faith

Scripture: *Hebrews 3:13* - "But encourage one another daily, as long as it is called 'Today,' so that none of you may be hardened by sin's deceitfulness." (NIV)

Reflection: One of the greatest ways you can support your siblings is by encouraging them in their faith. Pray with them, share what God is teaching you, and be there to help them through spiritual struggles. Encourage them to pursue God's purpose for their lives and remind them that God is always with them. Your support can make a big difference in their spiritual growth.

Journal Question: In what ways can you encourage your siblings in their walk with God?

Day 5: Being a Role Model for Siblings

Scripture: *1 Corinthians 11:1* - "Follow my example, as I follow the example of Christ." (NIV)

Reflection: Whether your siblings are older or younger than you, you have the opportunity to be a role model and set a positive example. Your actions, words, and attitude can influence how your siblings see God, relationships, and life. Strive to be a role model in all areas of your life, pointing your siblings to Jesus and showing them what it looks like to live a life that honors God.

Journal Question: Whether your siblings are younger or older, how can you be a positive role model for them?

Weekly Summary

This week, we explored what it means to be a good brother or sister — loving and supporting your siblings, handling rivalry with grace, encouraging them in their faith, and being a role model. God has placed you in each other's lives to walk together, love, and support each other through all seasons of life.

Real-Life Story

John and Charles Wesley: The Impact of a Brother's Encouragement One powerful example of a Christian who had a significant impact on their sibling's life is Charles Wesley and his brother John Wesley. Together, they were instrumental in founding the Methodist movement, but Charles's influence on John's spiritual journey and calling was profound.

Charles and John were both raised in a devout Christian home, but each struggled with finding assurance in their faith. In 1735, they traveled to the American colonies as missionaries, seeking to deepen their own understanding of God and help others. Despite their good intentions, they encountered personal failures and discouragement, feeling that their work had not fulfilled the spiritual renewal they sought. The trip left both brothers searching for a deeper connection with God. Shortly after returning to England, Charles experienced a powerful spiritual awakening. While reading Martin Luther's writings on the book of Galatians, he came to a profound understanding of grace and felt a newfound assurance of his faith in Christ. This experience transformed Charles, filling him with an unshakable confidence in God's love.

Charles shared this newfound faith with John, who was still struggling. With his brother's encouragement and testimony, John sought his own assurance of salvation. Just a few days later, John attended a meeting on Aldersgate Street in London, where he felt his "heart strangely warmed" and received the same sense of assurance in his faith. This experience became a pivotal moment in his life, leading him to pursue his calling with newfound zeal.

Together, the Wesley brothers went on to lead a revival in England that eventually spread worldwide. Charles's influence on John was vital in helping him find the spiritual assurance he needed to fulfill his calling, and their shared dedication to Christ changed countless lives. Charles, known as the "Sweet Singer of Methodism," wrote many hymns, while John became a passionate preacher and leader. Their legacy, built on the foundation of one brother's encouragement to another, continues to impact Christians to this day (Sprugeon, 2014).

Prayer

"God, thank You for my siblings and the special bond we share. Help me to be a good brother who loves, supports, and encourages them. Teach me to handle conflicts with grace and to be a positive role model that points them to You. Let my relationship with my siblings reflect Your love and strengthen our family bond. Amen."

ROMANTIC RELATIONSHIPS

Practical Challenge

If you are in a romantic relationship, take time to pray together and discuss ways to keep God at the center. If you are not dating, use this time to pray for God's guidance in future relationships and to focus on growing in your faith and character.

Day 1: God's Design for Love and Relationships

Scripture: *1 Corinthians 13:4-5* - "Love is patient and kind. Love is not jealous or boastful or proud or rude. It does not demand its own way. It is not irritable, and it keeps no record of being wronged." (NLT)

Reflection: God's design for love is based on selflessness, kindness, and respect. Romantic relationships should reflect this kind of love, where both people seek to honor God and each other. Love is not about what you can get from someone but how you can serve and uplift them. Keep God's design for love in mind as you consider and navigate relationships.

Journal Question: How does God's design for love differ from what the world often shows about romantic relationships?

Day 2: How to Keep God at the Center of a Relationship

Scripture: *Ecclesiastes 4:12* - "A person standing alone can be attacked and defeated, but two can stand back-to-back and conquer. Three are even better, for a triple-braided cord is not easily broken." (NLT)

Reflection: Keeping God at the center of a romantic relationship makes it stronger and healthier. When both you and the person you are dating are focused on honoring God, He becomes the "third strand" that holds you together. Pray together, seek God's will for your relationship, and encourage each other in your spiritual walks. Let God's presence be the foundation of your relationship.

Journal Question: What are some practical ways you can keep God at the center of your relationship or future relationships?

Day 3: Respecting Boundaries in Romantic Relationships

Scripture: *1 Thessalonians 4:3-4* - "God's will is for you to be holy, so stay away from all sexual sin. Then each of you will control his own body and live in holiness and honor—" (NLT)

Reflection: Setting and respecting boundaries in a romantic relationship is essential to honoring God and each other. Physical and emotional boundaries help you stay pure, build trust, and keep God's standards. Communicate openly with your significant other about the boundaries that are important to you, and commit to honoring them together. Instead of looking at boundaries in your relationship as something that divides you, approach setting those boundaries as a team. Work together to honor God's design for purity, sexuality, and marriage, even when it is difficult or inconvenient. You will see good fruit from honoring God's design.

Journal Question: Why are boundaries important in a relationship, and how can they help you honor God and each other?

Day 4: The Importance of Purity and Self-Control

Scripture: *2 Timothy 2:22* - "Run from anything that stimulates youthful lusts. Instead, pursue righteous living, faithfulness, love, and peace. Enjoy the companionship of those who call on the Lord with pure hearts." (NLT)

Reflection: Purity isn't just about what you avoid; it's about what you pursue. God calls you to pursue righteousness, faith, love, and peace, living in a way that honors Him. Practicing self-control in your thoughts, actions, and relationships helps you walk in purity. Seek God's strength to make choices that reflect His holiness, and surround yourself with people who encourage you to stay pure.

Journal Question: How can you practice purity and self-control in your thoughts, actions, and relationships?

Day 5: Navigating Dating with Wisdom and Faith

Scripture: *2 Corinthians 6:14* - "Do not be yoked together with unbelievers. For what do righteousness and wickedness have in common? Or what fellowship can light have with darkness?" (NIV)

Reflection: God wants you to pursue relationships that honor Him and encourage spiritual growth. Being "unequally yoked" means being in a close relationship — like dating — with someone who doesn't share your faith. This can lead to conflicts in values and make it difficult to keep God at the center. Trust God to bring someone into your life who shares your faith and will encourage you to grow closer to Him.

Journal Question: What are some qualities you should seek in a person you date, and how can you trust God's timing and guidance in your love life?

Weekly Summary

This week, we discussed God's design for romantic relationships, keeping God at the center, respecting boundaries, living in purity, and navigating dating with wisdom and faith. Romantic relationships are meant to reflect God's love, honor Him, and encourage spiritual growth. Trust God's plan for your love life and let Him lead you toward a relationship that honors Him.

Real-Life Story

Jeremy and Melissa Camp: A Love That Honored God Through Suffering
Christian musician Jeremy Camp married his first wife, Melissa, knowing she had terminal cancer. They chose to honor God through their short marriage, trusting Him even in the midst of suffering. Though Melissa passed away just months after their wedding, her faith and their commitment to God left a powerful legacy. Jeremy wrote the song "I Still Believe" during this difficult season, expressing his continued trust in God. Their story is a reminder that God-centered relationships are built on faith, trust, and love that go beyond circumstances. Even in heartbreak, Jeremy and Melissa's love reflected God's grace and purpose (Camp, 2020).

Prayer

"Dear God, thank You for Your design for love and relationships. Help me to keep You at the center of my relationships, to respect boundaries, and to live in purity. Give me wisdom as I navigate dating and trust Your guidance in my love life. Let my relationships honor You and reflect Your love. Amen."

REFLECTING ON THE JOURNEY

Practical Challenge

Spend some time in prayer this week, reflecting on the past year and setting goals for your spiritual journey moving forward. Ask God to continue to guide you, help you grow, and draw you closer to Him in the year to come. Pick a book from the **Resources for Further Study** at the end of this book to dive deeper into another faithful believer's story to help encourage you in your walk.

Day 1: Reviewing Your Growth Over the Past Year

Scripture: *Philippians 1:6* - "And I am certain that God, who began the good work within you, will continue his work until it is finally finished on the day when Christ Jesus returns." (NLT)

Reflection: This past year has been a journey of growth, learning, and drawing closer to God. Take time to reflect on how God has been at work in your life, shaping your heart and growing your faith. Remember that the work

God has started in you will continue as you walk with Him. Celebrate how far you've come, and trust that God will carry you forward.

Journal Question: How have you grown in your faith and relationship with God over the past year?

Day 2: Thanking God for His Guidance and Help

Scripture: *Psalm 100:4* - "Enter into His gates with thanksgiving, *and* into His courts with praise. Be thankful to Him, *and* bless His name." (NKJV)

Reflection: Gratitude is a fitting way to end this year-long journey. Thank God for His guidance, help, and faithfulness through every season. Whether you faced challenges or experienced great joys, God has been with you every step of the way. Let your heart overflow with thanksgiving as you remember His goodness and reflect on all that He has done.

Journal Question: What challenges or blessings has God used to shape you, and how can you thank Him for His faithfulness?

Day 3: Identifying Areas of Continued Growth

Scripture: *Romans 2:6-8* - "God 'will repay each person according to what they have done.' To those who by persistence in doing good seek glory, honor and immortality, he will give eternal life. But for those who are self-seeking and who reject the truth and follow evil, there will be wrath and anger." (NIV)

Reflection: Even though you've grown a lot, there are still areas where God is calling you to continue growing. Identify the areas of your life where you still need to develop spiritually, whether it's in your habits, character, or relationships. Ask God to help you run the race with perseverance, removing anything that hinders your growth and pressing on toward His purpose for you.

Journal Question: What areas of your life do you still need to grow in, and how can you continue to pursue spiritual maturity?

Day 4: Setting Goals for Your Spiritual Journey Moving Forward

Scripture: *Proverbs 16:9* - "A man's heart plans his way, but the Lord directs his steps." (NKJV)

Reflection: As you reflect on what God has done in your life this past year, take time to set goals for your spiritual journey moving forward. Think about how you want to grow in your faith, your relationship with God, and your service to others. Pray for God's guidance as you plan, and trust that He will establish your steps in His timing and purpose.

Journal Question: What spiritual goals would you like to set for the coming year, and how can you ask God to guide your path?

Day 5: Committing to Keep Growing in Your Relationship with God

Scripture: *Jeremiah 29:13* - "And you will seek Me and find *Me*, when you search for Me with all your heart." (NKJV)

Reflection: Growing in your relationship with God is a lifelong journey, and He promises that when you seek Him with all your heart, you will find Him. Commit to continue pursuing God, seeking His presence, and growing in your faith. Let this year be just the beginning of a deeper, more meaningful relationship with your Heavenly Father.

Journal Question: How can you commit to keep seeking God with all your heart as you move forward?

Weekly Summary

This week, we focused on reflecting on the past year, thanking God for His guidance, identifying areas for continued growth, setting spiritual goals, and committing to keep growing in your relationship with God. As you look back on all that God has done and look ahead to the future, let your heart be filled with gratitude, hope, and a desire to keep seeking Him.

Real-Life Story

Oswald Chambers: A Lifelong Pursuit of Spiritual Growth Oswald Chambers, the Scottish minister and teacher best known for his devotional work *My Utmost for His Highest*, had a profound commitment to personal spiritual growth throughout his life. One notable story that exemplifies this pursuit occurred during his time as a student at the Royal School of Mines in London. Initially, Chambers had aspirations to become a painter and enrolled in the school to study art. However, during his time there, he experienced a transformative moment that shifted the trajectory of his life toward a deeper exploration of faith and spirituality. Influenced by a group of Christian friends and a growing interest in the teachings of Jesus, Chambers began to feel a strong call to ministry. This transition was not merely about a change in career; it represented a profound inner awakening. Oswald sought to understand God's will for his life, which prompted him to delve deeply into the Scriptures and engage in prayerful reflection. He would spend hours in contemplation, seeking to deepen his relationship with God and discern His purpose for him.

One of the pivotal moments in Chambers's pursuit of spiritual growth came when he attended a Bible conference led by the evangelist D. L. Moody. Moody's powerful preaching had a lasting impact on Chambers and confirmed his desire to serve God more fully. Inspired by this experience, Chambers made a conscious decision to dedicate his life to ministry, embracing the teachings of Christ with passion and fervor. To further his spiritual development, Chambers also immersed himself in the study of theology, church history, and the writings of other Christian thinkers. He was particularly influenced by the teachings of John Wesley, the founder of Methodism, who emphasized the importance of personal holiness and the pursuit of a deeper relationship with God. Chambers adopted these principles and integrated them into his own spiritual practices.

Despite his commitment to growth, Chambers faced challenges, including doubts and struggles with his own weaknesses. However, he remained steadfast in his pursuit, believing that personal growth was a lifelong journey marked by both triumphs and failures. He often wrote about the necessity of humility and dependence on God in his devotional works, encouraging others to embrace their own journeys of faith. Chambers eventually became a popular speaker and teacher, known for his deep insights and ability to articulate the complexities of faith. His writings continue to inspire countless individuals seeking to grow spiritually and develop a closer relationship with God. Through his own journey of personal spiritual growth, Oswald Chambers left a lasting legacy that challenges believers to pursue their faith with sincerity, dedication, and a willingness to learn from both their successes and failures.

Prayer

"God, thank You for guiding me through this past year and helping me grow in my relationship with You. Help me to reflect on all You've done, to set goals for my spiritual journey, and to commit to seeking You with all my heart. Continue to shape me, lead me, and draw me closer to You in the days ahead. Amen."

Resources for Further Study

Below is a list of books, websites, and resources where you can find more information about the individuals featured in the **Real-Life Story** sections of each week. These men and women have lived out their faith in powerful ways, and their stories provide great inspiration and encouragement as you grow in your own walk with God.

Week 1: Eric Liddell

- *Book: Pure Gold: Eric Liddell – An Olympic Champion's Legacy* by David McCasland

- *Website:* https://ericliddell.org/about-eric-liddell/

Week 2: Katie Davis Majors

- *Book: Kisses from Katie: A Story of Relentless Love and Redemption* by Katie J. Davis

- *Website:* https://katiedavismajors.com/

Week 3: Bilquis Sheikh

- *Book: I Dared to Call Him Father* by Bilquis Sheikh

- *Website:* https://peoplepill.com/i/bilquis-sheikh#google_vignette

Week 4: George Müller

- *Book: The Autobiography of George Müller* by George Müller

- *Website:* https://www.georgemuller.org/

Week 5: Brother Lawrence

- *Book: The Practice of the Presence of God* by Brother Lawrence

- *Website:* https://canonjjohn.com/2022/10/08/heroes-of-the-faith-brother-lawrence/

Week 6, 27: Elisabeth Elliot

- *Book: Passion and Purity: Learning to Bring Your Love Life Under Christ's Control* by Elisabeth Elliot

- *Website:* https://elisabethelliot.org/

Week 7, 36: Dietrich Bonhoeffer

- *Book: The Cost of Discipleship* by Dietrich Bonhoeffer

- *Website:* https://bonhoeffersociety.org/about/bonhoeffer/biography/

Week 8: Matt Redman

- *Website*: https://acsirevivals.wordpress.com/articles/heart-of-worship-matt-redman-story-behind-it/

- *Website:* https://www.youtube.com/watch?v=m83TSHhg-jU

Week 9: William Booth

- *Book: William and Catherine: The Life and Legacy of the Booths, Founders of the Salvation Army* by Trevor Yaxley

- *Website:* https://www.salvationarmy.org.uk/about-us/international-heritage-centre/virtual-heritage-centre/people/william-booth

Week 10: Joni Eareckson Tada

- *Book: Joni: An Unforgettable Story* by Joni Eareckson Tada

- *Website:* https://joniandfriends.org/

Week 11, 23: Hudson Taylor

- *Book: Hudson Taylor's Spiritual Secret* by Dr. & Mrs. Howard Taylor

- *Website:* https://omf.org/james-hudson-taylor-founder-of-cim-omf-international/

Week 12: David Wilkerson

- *Book: The Cross and the Switchblade* by Rev. David Wilkerson

- *Website:* https://tsc.nyc/david-wilkerson/

Week 13, 34: Billy Graham

- *Book: Just As I Am: The Autobiography of Billy Graham* by Billy Graham

- *Book: The Holy Spirit: Activating God's Power in Your Life* by Billy Graham

- *Website:* https://billygraham.org/

Week 14: C.S. Lewis

- *Book: Mere Christianity* by C.S. Lewis

- *Website:* https://www.cslewis.com/us/

Week 15: Smith Wigglesworth

- *Book: Smith Wigglesworth on the Holy Spirit* by Smith Wigglesworth

- *Website:* https://smithwigglesworth.com/life-in-the-spirit/

Week 16: John Newton

- *Book: Out of the Depths: The Autobiography of John Newton* by John Newton

- *Website:* https://christianhistoryinstitute.org/magazine/article/amazingly-graced-john-newton

Week 17: Brother Andrew

- *Book: God's Smuggler* by Andrew van der Bijl, Elizabeth Sherrill, and John Sherrill

- *Website:* https://www.opendoorsuk.org/about/our-history/brother-andrew/

Week 18, 47: Nick Vujicic

- *Book: Life Without Limits: Inspiration for a Ridiculously Good Life* by Nick Vujicic

- *Website:* https://nickvministries.org/

Week 19: Christine Cain

- *Book: Unashamed: Drop the Baggage, Pick up Your Freedom, Fulfill Your Destiny* by Christine Caine

- *Website:* https://christinecaine.com/

Week 20: Lecrae

- *Book: I Am Restored: How I Lost My Religion but Found My Faith* by Lecrae

- *Website:* https://www.lifeway.com/en/articles/lecrae-unashamed-from-rehab-to-redemption?

Week 21: Max Lucado

- *Book: Anxious for Nothing: Finding Calm in a Chaotic World* by Max Lucado

- *Website:* https://maxlucado.com/

Week 22: Tim Tebow

- *Book: Shaken: Discovering Your True Identity in the Midst of Life's Storms* by Tim Tebow

- *Website:* https://timtebowfoundation.org/

Week 24, 39: Sadie Robertson Huff

- *Book: Live: remain alive, be alive at a specified time, have an exciting or fulfilling life* by Sadie Robertson and Beth Clark

- *Website:* https://liveoriginal.com/about/

Week 25: Lottie Moon

- *Book: The Life and Letters of Lottie Moon* by Lottie Moon

- *Website:* https://www.imb.org/about/lottie-moon/

Week 26: Bethany Hamilton

- *Book: Soul Surfer: A True Story of Faith, Family, and Fighting to Get Back on the Board* by Bethany Hamilton

- *Website:* https://bethanyhamilton.com/

Week 28: Samantha Ponder

- *Book: The Samantha Ponder Story: From Sideline Reporter to Football Countdown Host, Discover the Inspiring Journey of a Trailblazing Sportscaster Who Redefined Sports Media* by Regina Sharp

- *Website:* https://www.fca.org/fca-in-action/blog-detail/2017/11/06/6-questions-with-samantha-ponder

Week 29: Walt Disney

- *Book: The Man Behind the Magic: The Story of Walt Disney* by Catherine and Richard Greene

- *Website:* https://www.biography.com/movies-tv/walt-disney-failures

Week 30: William Carey

- *Book: The Legacy of William Carey: A Model for the Transformation of a Culture* by Vishal and Ruth Mangalwadi

- *Website:* https://www.imb.org/2018/07/31/missionaries-you-should-know-william-carey/

Week 31: David Green

- *Book: Giving It All Away...and Getting It All Back Again: The Way of Living Generously* by David Green

- *Website:* https://www.youtube.com/watch?v=2mjOHi-xDE8

Week 32, 42: Corrie ten Boom

- *Book: Tramp for the Lord* by Corrie ten Boom

- *Book: The Hiding Place* by Corrie ten Boom

- *Website:* https://www.corrietenboom.com/en/family-ten-boom

Week 33: J.C. Penney

- *Book: Fifty Years With the Golden Rule: A Spiritual Autobiography* by J.C. Penney

- *Website:* https://www.christianity.com/church/church-history/timeline/1901-2000/jc-penney-11630672.html

Week 35: Jim Elliot

- *Book: Shadow of the Almighty: The Life and Testament of Jim Elliot* by Elisabeth Elliot

- *Website:* https://www.christianity.com/church/church-history/timeline/1901-2000/jim-elliot-no-fool-11634862.html

Week 37: William Wilberforce and John Newton

- *Book: Amazing grace: William Wilberforce and the Heroic Campaign to End Slavery* by Eric Metaxas

- *Website:* https://washingtoninst.org/mentoring-a-georgian-era-daniel-john-newton-and-william-wilberforce/

Week 38: William Carey and Andrew Fuller

- *Book: William Carey: Obliged to Go* by Janet and Geoff Benge

- *Website:* https://banneroftruth.org/us/about/banner-authors/andrew-fuller/?

Week 40: Truett Cathy

- *Book: Wealth: Is It Worth It?* by Truett Cathy

- *Website:* https://time.com/3310038/rick-warren-chick-fil-a-founder-truett-cathy-truly-lived-his-faith/

Week 41: Tony Dungy

- *Book: Quiet Strength: The Principles, Practices, and Priorities of a Winning Life* by Tony Dungy with Nathan Whitaker

- *Website:* https://coachdungy.com/

Week 43: Mother Teresa

- *Book: Mother Teresa: Come Be My Light* by Mother Teresa

- *Website:* https://www.biography.com/religious-figures/mother-teresa

Week 44: Martin Luther King Jr.

- *Book: Strength to Love* by Martin Luther King Jr.

- *Website:* https://thekingcenter.org/about-tkc/martin-luther-king-jr/

Week 45: Fred Rogers

- *Book: The World According to Mister Rogers: Important Things to Remember* by Fred Rogers
- *Website:* https://www.dougdickerson.net/2019/06/30/leadership-lessons-from-fred-rogers/

Week 46: William and Catherine Booth

- *Book: The Life & Ministry of William Booth: Founder of The Salvation Army* by Roger J. Green
- *Website:* https://www.salvationarmy.org.uk/about-us/international-heritage-centre/virtual-heritage-centre/people/william-booth

Week 48: Abraham Lincoln

- *Book: Lincoln's Devotional: The Believer's Daily Treasure* by Abraham Lincoln
- *Website:* https://www.abrahamlincolnonline.org/lincoln/speeches/faithquotes.htm

Week 49: Henri Nouwen

- *Book: Henri Nouwen and Spiritual Direction: Wisdom for the Long Walk of Faith* by Henri Nouwen
- *Website:* https://www.americamagazine.org/faith/2016/10/05/spirituality-henri-nouwen-qa-gabrielle-earnshaw

Week 50: John and Charles Wesley

- *Book: John and Charles Wesley: Selections from Their Writings and Hymns* by Frank Whaling
- *Website:* https://www.christianitytoday.com/2008/08/john-wesley/
- *Website:* https://hymnary.org/person/Wesley_Charles

Week 51: Jeremy Camp & Melissa Camp

- *Book: I Still Believe* by Jeremy Camp

- *Website:* https://www.youtube.com/watch?v=5FMmxKM5Wj0

Week 52: Oswald Chambers

- *Book: My Utmost for His Highest* by Oswald Chambers

- *Website:* https://utmost.org/

These resources provide deeper insights into the lives of people who lived with boldness, faith, and love for God. Their stories can inspire you to live out your own faith with courage and commitment.

Feel free to explore these books and websites to learn more about the faith journeys, struggles, and victories of these incredible individuals. May their examples encourage you as you continue on your own walk with Christ.

Reference

ACS International. (n.d.). *Heart of worship - Matt Redman's story behind it.* ACS International Revivals. Retrieved from https://acsirevivals.wordpress.com/articles/heart-of-worship-matt-redman-story-behind-it/

Billy Graham Evangelistic Association. (n.d.). *Billy Graham Quotes.*

Bonhoeffer, D. (2001). *Ethics* (K. W. Gros, Ed.). Fortress Press. (Original work published 1949)

Booth, W. (1890). *In darkest England and the way out.* Salvation Army.

Brooks, D. (2018, July 6). *Fred Rogers and the loveliness of the little good.* The New York Times. .

Brother Andrew, & Sherrill, J. (1967). *God's smuggler.* Chosen Books.

Caine, C. (2016). *Unashamed: Drop the baggage, pick up your freedom, fulfill your destiny.* Zondervan.

Camp, J. (2020). *I still believe: A memoir.* Thomas Nelson.

Cannon, M. L. (1997). *Lottie Moon: A biography of the revered missionary to China.* Broadman & Holman Publishers.

Carey, W. (1792). *An enquiry into the obligations of Christians, to use means for the conversion of the heathens.* Leicester.

Carwardine, R. (2007). *Lincoln: A life of purpose and power.* Vintage.

Cathy, T. (2007). *How did you do it, Truett?: A Recipe for Success.* Looking Glass Books, Inc.

Chambers, O. (2017). *My utmost for his highest.* Discovery House Publishers.

Curry, Izola Ware. The Martin Luther King, Jr. Research and Education Institute. (n.d.). .

Davis Majors, K. (2012). *Kisses from Katie: A story of relentless love and redemption.* Howard Books.

Dungy, T. (2008). *Quiet strength: The principles, practices, and priorities of a winning life.* Tyndale Momentum.

Elliot, E. (1989). *The gate of splendor.* Revell.

Elliot, E. (1989). *Shadow of the Almighty: The life and testament of Jim Elliot.* HarperOne. (Original work published 1958)

Elliot, E. (2003). *Passion and purity: Learning to bring your love life under Christ's control.* Revell.

Graham, B. (1997). *Just as I am: The autobiography of Billy Graham.* HarperOne.

Graham, B. (2006). *The Journey: How to live by faith in an uncertain world.* Thomas Nelson.

Green, R.J. (2006). *The life & ministry of william booth: Founder of the salvation army.* Abingdon Press.

Greene, D. (2017). *Purpose over profit: How owning a business can change the world.* WaterBrook.

Greene, K., & Greene, H. (2016). *The man behind the magic: The story of Walt Disney.* Disney Editions.

Hamilton, B. (2004). *Soul surfer: A true story of faith, family, and fighting to get back on the board.* MTV Books.

Harris, L. (Correspondent). (2013). *The Chapel Hill News, Section: Chapel Hill News, Column: My View: Kindness makes a community.* Quote Page 1A. NewsBank Access World News.

Huff, S. R. (2020). *Live: Remain alive, be alive at a specified time, have an exciting or fulfilling life.* Thomas Nelson.

Jones, O. A. (1971). *J.C. Penney: The man with a thousand partners.* Ayer Company Publishers.

King, M. L., Jr. (2012). *A Gift of love: Sermons from "strength to love" and other preachings.* Beacon Press.

Lawrence, B. (1982). *The practice of the presence of God.* Spire Books. (Original work published 1692)

Lecrae. (2020). *I am restored: How I lost my religion but found my faith.* Zondervan.

Lewis, C. S. (1955). *Surprised by joy: The shape of my early life.* Harcourt Brace.

Liddell, E. (2001). *Pure gold: Eric Liddell – An Olympic champion's legacy.* Discovery House.

Lucado, M. (2017). *Anxious for nothing: Finding calm in a chaotic world.* Thomas Nelson.

McCasland, D. (1998). *Oswald Chambers: Abandoned to God: The life story of the author of my utmost for is highest.* Our Daily Bread Publishing.

Metaxas, E. (2007). *Amazing grace: William Wilberforce and the heroic campaign to end slavery.* HarperOne.

Metaxas, E. (2010). *Bonhoeffer: Pastor, martyr, prophet, spy.* Thomas Nelson.

Müller, G. (1984). *The autobiography of George Müller.* Whitaker House.

Newton, J. (2003). *Out of the depths: The autobiography of John Newton.* Kregel Publications.

Nobel Prize Outreach AB 2024. (November 2024) *Mother Teresa – Acceptance Speech.* NobelPrize.org.

O'Laughlin, M. (2009). *Henri Nouwen: His life and vision.* Orbis Books.

Piper, J. (2016). *Andrew Fuller: Holy faith, worthy gospel, world mission.* Crossway.

Pullinger, J. (2006). *Chasing the dragon: One woman's struggle against the darkness of Hong Kong's drug dens.* Hodder & Stoughton.

Redman, M. (2002). *The Unquenchable worshipper: Coming back to the heart of worship.* Regal Books.

Sharp, R. (2024). *The Samantha Ponder story: From sideline reporter to football countdown host, discover the inspiring journey of a trailblazing sportscaster who redefined sports media.* Amazon Digital Services LLC-Kdp.

Sheikh, B., & Schneider, R. (1978). *I dared to call Him Father: The miraculous story of a Muslim woman's encounter with God.* Chosen Books.

Sprugeon, C. H. (2014) *The two Wesleys: On John and Charles Wesley.* Wipf and Stock.

Tada, J. E. (1976). *Joni: An unforgettable story.* Zondervan.

Tada, J. E. (2010). *A place of healing: Wrestling with the mysteries of suffering, pain, and God's sovereignty.* David C. Cook.

Taylor, H., & Taylor, M. (1997). *Hudson Taylor's spiritual secret.* Moody Publishers. (Original work published 1911)

Tebow, T., & Whitaker, A. (2016). *Shaken: Discovering your true identity in the midst of life's storms.* WaterBrook.

Ten Boom, C. (1974). *Tramp for the Lord.* Chosen Books.

Ten Boom, C. (1982). *Clippings from my notebook.* Thomas Nelson Inc.

Ten Boom, C. (2006). *The hiding place.* Chosen Books.

Vujicic, N. (2010). *Life without limits: Inspiration for a ridiculously good life.* Doubleday.

Wigglesworth, S. (2002). *Smith Wigglesworth on the Holy Spirit.* Whitaker House.

Wilkerson, D. (1963). *The Cross and the switchblade.* Jove Books.

William Carey International Development. (n.d.). *William Carey Quotes.* https://www.facebook.com/WCIDJ/

Acknowledgments:

This devotional was developed with the help of various tools and resources, including OpenAI's ChatGPT for assisting in organizing and generating ideas, reflections, and content.

Made in the USA
Las Vegas, NV
13 August 2025

26281420R00134